BEGINNER'S GUIDE TO

Calligraphy

BEGINNER'S GUIDE TO
Calligraphy

Marie Lynskey

Sterling Publishing Co., Inc.
New York

Creative director: Sarah King
Editor: Clare Haworth-Maden
Project editor: Judith Millidge
Designer: Axis Design Editions

Library of Congress Cataloging-in-Publication Data Available

10   9   8   7   6   5   4   3   2   1

Published in 2003 by Sterling Publishing Co. Inc.
387 Park Avenue South
New York, N.Y. 10016

First published in 2001 under the title A Beginner's Art Guide: Calligraphy
by D&S Books Ltd
Kerswell, Parkham Ash
Bideford, Devon, EX39 5PR

© 2000 D&S Books Ltd

Distributed in Canada by Sterling Publishing
c/o Canadian Manda Group,
One Atlantic Avenue, Suite 105
Toronto, Ontario, Canada M6K 3E7, Canada

Printed in China

Sterling ISBN 1-4027-0878-5

Contents

Introduction

Mass-produced and quickly discarded things have become commonplace in our lives today, with the result that handwritten and hand-painted documents that have been created with more thought, time, and attention have become increasingly precious and worthy of a place in our busy lives. Because the printed word on the page or computer screen is forever before us, it is a refreshing change and a great satisfaction to those who appreciate their value to be able to produce and view decorative lettering that has been prepared with time and care simply for the pleasure that it gives.

Fig. 1. Reconstruction of cuneiform lettering on clay tablet.

The History of Writing

We can trace the history of writing back to ancient times, to the cuneiform script of the Sumerians over 5000 years ago. Clay tablets were used, the images being pressed into the damp clay, which was then baked hard. Many tablets of this sort have been discovered (Fig. 1).

The word cuneiform actually means "wedge-shaped," as the tools employed for making the information impressed the clay with small, wedge-shaped marks, tapering from a wide start to a thin, pointed end. The earliest images were attempts to describe pictorially the information that the writer was trying to convey, but a more contained selection of symbols gradually came to be adopted, which represented spoken sounds rather than things. Although this set of symbols was eventually reduced in number as the centuries went by, it was still far from reaching today's alphabet of 26 letters. The cuneiform script spread with the conquering of Sumeria by the Babylonians, who in turn were overtaken by the Assyrians. The script was adopted by conquering peoples and was dispersed by fleeing native peoples, causing it to spread throughout the Middle East.

The Egyptians were developing their writing skills at the same time as the Sumerians, but they advanced farther by developing a smaller series of symbols. Their hieroglyphics (the word means "sacred engraved writing") were essentially picture-writing systems, and the use of a reed brush or pen and papyrus made the task simpler than the Sumerians' clay tablets (Fig.2). Egyptian scribes used black ink made from carbon mixed with water and gum and red ink made with a natural, red-earth pigment mixed in the same way.

Papyrus is made from the pith of reeds grown in Egypt; it is kept in rolls and is only written upon on one side, the other not being suitable for lettering (Fig. 3). Papyrus is constructed by removing the outer covering of the papyrus reed and cutting the inner pith into thin layers. These strips are laid side by side lengthwise, with the edges overlapping slightly. A second layer of strips is placed on top, at right angles to the first row. Next the layers are beaten flat, to remove some of the moisture. The papyrus is then left to dry under pressure in order to keep it flat and smooth, and the natural adhesive in the plant binds the strips together to form a single sheet.

The Egyptians clung to their pictorial writing long after some of their neighbors had begun to devise more efficient writing systems that consisted of fewer symbols. The Phoenicians adopted a style that owed its beginnings to both cuneiform and hieroglyphics, developing an alphabet that contained a similar number of letters to those that we now use (Fig. 4).

It is from them that the Greeks may have developed their writing techniques, adapting the Phoenician letters and incor-

Fig.2. Reconstructed hieroglyphics on papyrus.

Fig. 3. Papyrus, made of overlapping strips of papyrus reed, and reed pen.

Fig. 4. Phoenician letters.

porating signs to represent their own sounds. The angular letters of some Greek lettering styles (Fig. 5) may have been due to the use of a wax tablet; it is easier to form straight lines when writing in wax with an iron or wooden stylus. The wax tablet was a wooden tray with a small lip round the edge and a coating of a thin layer of wax over the inner surface. Once the tablet was written upon, the letters could be easily erased by slightly melting and then smoothing out the wax again.

As papyrus became more expensive and difficult to obtain as a result of the deterioration of the Mediterranean trade routes and Rome's decline in power, vellum and parchment began to replace it. Vellum is the specially prepared skin of calves or goats, while parchment is the skin of sheep. The surface of both is very smooth and easy to write upon, and the sheets could either be white or cream, with slight, but attractive, vein markings running through the skins. Leather had been used as a writing surface by Hebrew scribes, who wrote from right to left, and it is thought that vellum was first produced in Pergamum in Asia Minor (the German word for vellum is *Pergament*, which seems to bear out this theory).

Roman lettering followed on from the Greek, and the Latin alphabets varied from very precisely drawn capitals, such as the quadrata, or square-capital, alphabet that was carved on stone (Fig. 6), to such more free-flowing, quickly written styles as rustica (Fig. 7), which was used in documents. These styles spread throughout the Roman Empire. Vellum furthermore brought about the construction of books, whereas papyrus had been rolled up.

The quill pen was also devised and became a well-used writing instrument. Quills are much more flexible than reed pens, and as a consequence the styles that were written with them evolved accordingly (see page 18 for instructions on making your own quill pen).

Arabic scripts were also derived from the Phoenicians' system, culminating in the writing of the Koran, which standardized the script during the early seventh century. It spread rapidly throughout the regions that were conquered by the Arabs, but its spread toward Western Europe was halted by Arab defeats at the hands of the Franks. Some of the earliest writing on vellum is Arabic (Fig. 8).

Fig. 5. Greek letters.

Fig. 6. Quadrata capitals.

RVSTICA

C. CVSPIVM.

Fig. 7. Rustica capitals.

كي طلك ء امشت نه بس وزكآر

Fig. 8. Arabic writing on vellum.

Chinese lettering dates from at least 1000 B.C., and developed in much the same way as cuneiform, using picture forms, but in vertical columns—indeed, it still follows this method (Fig. 9). We are indebted to the Chinese for their invention of paper in about A.D. 100 (they had previously used wood, bamboo, and silk as writing surfaces, but paper came to be regarded the most practical material). Its use gradually spread, first to Japan and eventually toward the West, progressing via the Islamic countries to Spain and the rest of Europe. One of the earliest-known European manuscripts to have been written on paper is a deed of King Roger of Sicily dated 1109, whose text is written in both Arabic and Greek. Paper was being used in England from the mid-thirteenth century, but paper manufacture did not begin in England until the end of the fifteenth century, when a small paper mill was set up in Hertfordshire by John Tate. Another two centuries would pass before its use became widespread and it supplanted vellum as the principal writing surface.

The Development of Lettering Styles

Returning to late Roman lettering, a script known as uncial was developed and used in Roman books (Fig. 10), which later became the script of the Celtic monasteries as missionaries dispersed throughout Europe spreading Christianity, which had become the official religion of Rome during the fourth century. The Romans wrote on vellum with quill pens, and it was possible to achieve a much finer quality of letter with these precisely cut writing instruments.

With the breakup of the Roman Empire during the fifth century, widespread communications deteriorated and it was largely the Roman Catholic Church that kept arts and learning alive throughout the Dark Ages. The uncial script was adopted by Christian scribes and became the dominant book hand in the West from the fifth to eighth centuries. Christians required texts that explained their religion to enable them to spread their message, and the Greek word *biblos* describes their primary book, or Bible, which was copied, recopied, and illuminated on an ever-increasing scale. The production of Christian illuminated manuscripts thrived in isolated parts of Europe, and the seventh and eighth centuries saw the creation of some of the most complex and attractive manuscripts ever produced in what became known as the insular style. Missionaries and monks took books with them on their travels and thus encouraged the spread of different lettering styles throughout Europe. The books were lent and copied (this was the only means of acquiring a new book), and many medieval manuscripts depict monks at work, their writing materials and paints being clearly visible.

Although the uncial alphabet consisted of majuscule (capital) letters, a minuscule (small) alphabet was also beginning to emerge. The uncial hand deteriorated toward the ninth century, its spaciousness and formality being replaced by a more quickly written and economically spaced style. A mixture of the formal uncial that was used in great works and the more cursive versions that were used in informal writings gradually came to be known as the half-uncial script (Fig.11).

Fig. 9. Chinese lettering.

UNCIAL

HAECITAAPUT

Fig. 10. Uncial letters.

half uncial

nobir cunae fuid

Fig. 11. Half-uncial letters.

carolingian

noftri inlucam

Fig. 12. Carolingian letters.

merouingian

fid omne cdnfufum

Fig. 13. Merovingian letters.

anglo – raxon

defringulir bonomi

dirputa; red alththinir

Fig. 15. Anglo-saxon letters.

virigothic

nomineaheudimer q

Fig. 16. Visigothic letters.

gothic

Op lyn houet

Fig. 18. Gothic letters.

textura

Nota in aduentu

Fig. 19. Textura letters.

insular

iohannis furrexit

Fig. 14. Insular letters.

beneventan

quae lam nonptopa

Fig. 17. Beneventan letters.

rotunda

œuli domini fuper

Fig. 20. Rotunda letters.

The next major style was developed as a result of the Holy Roman Emperor Charlemagne's wish to promote learning. Charlemagne, the king of the Franks who lived from 742 to 814, gave his name to the Carolingian script (Fig.12), which had long ascending and descending stokes to the letters and a free-flowing, elegant style. Charlemagne's patronage of the arts brought about the widespread adoption of minuscule alphabets, and we can trace the formation of a series of closely related styles throughout Europe.

In France, there was the Merovingian style (Fig.13), which was named after the dynasty that preceded Charlemagne's. An insular style of lettering (Fig. 14) continued to develop in Northern Britain and was not superseded by the Carolingian until the mid-tenth century. Anglo-Saxon lettering (Fig. 15), which was influenced by Roman missionaries, was introduced by monks from England to continental Europe.

The Spanish Visigothic (Fig. 16) was a style that survived into the twelfth century, while the Beneventan script(Fig. 17) evolved in Monte Cassino in Southern Italy during the ninth century and survived into the thirteenth century. All of these lettering styles thrived in Europe, and were used in the manuscripts that were produced in various centers of learning throughout the early Middle Ages.

The thirteenth century saw the emergence of the Gothic scripts (Fig. 18), whereby the rounded letter shapes that had been used during the previous centuries became gradually more angular, culminating in the textura script (Fig. 19) of the fourteenth century, with its dense, black covering of vertical lines connected by thin, hairline strokes. Richly decorated Gothic manuscripts, illuminated with gold leaf and reflecting the extravagant fashions, courtly life, and romantic ideals that were popular at the time, were produced for great patrons of the arts. In Italy, the rotunda style (Fig. 20), which represented a return to a more rounded version of the Gothic hand, found favor, particularly in music books. The Gothic styles took up much less space than the Carolingian hands, which enabled more text to be fitted into a page. Gothic was the first lettering style to appear in the printed books that were first produced during the fifteenth century. As a result, slowly produced, handwritten books began to decline in numbers, while increasingly widely available printed books carried the written word to classes of people who had never before had the chance to possess it.

An attractive style known as bastarda (Fig. 21) bridged the gap to the next major changes in lettering styles that were brought about by the Renaissance. Bastarda was a cursive amalgamation and adaptation of the Gothic and Carolingian styles that appeared in Europe during the fifteenth century. The letters are quite curved, but with angular points at the top and bottom. Although it was adapted as an informal writing style, some beautiful formal examples can be found in the form of official documents and poetry, although not religious documents.

Italy spearheaded the introduction of the Renaissance lettering styles, which represented attempts by scholars to return to the simpler styles that had preceded the Gothic scripts. Such styles as the Carolingian were used as models, but the new styles had a gradual tendency to slope to the right and to become increasingly cursive, no doubt in the interests of speed. This italic hand, as it became known, soon became very popular and widespread. Cancelleresca, which had a neat, formal appearance, was one form of italic script that emerged (Fig. 22), while another, the humanistic hand (Fig. 23), had a neat, clear-cut precision to its letters and evolved as a result of the study of antiquarian Roman styles.

With the widespread production of printed books, we finally arrive at the copperplate style (Fig. 24), which was first formed by the action of the engraver's burin—an engraving tool with a sharp point—on printing plates. Interestingly, the terms "lower case," which is often applied to minuscule letters, and "upper case," which describes majuscule or capital letters, are derived from the cases, or drawers, in which printers kept their different sets of type. Copperplate came to be used to form fantastically flourished lettering, sometimes embellished almost to the point of illegibility. When written with a fine-pointed pen and ink, the letters could be very beautiful, and it was the copperplate script that filled the copybooks that many writing masters used to teach handwriting. From the beginning of the nineteenth century, steel pens began to be produced and manufactured in quantity; these had the advantage over quill pens of ease of acquisition and greater durability and consequently became widely used.

Fig. 21. Bastarda letters.

Fig. 22. Cancelleresca letters.

Fig. 23. Humanistic letters.

Fig. 24. Copperplate letters.

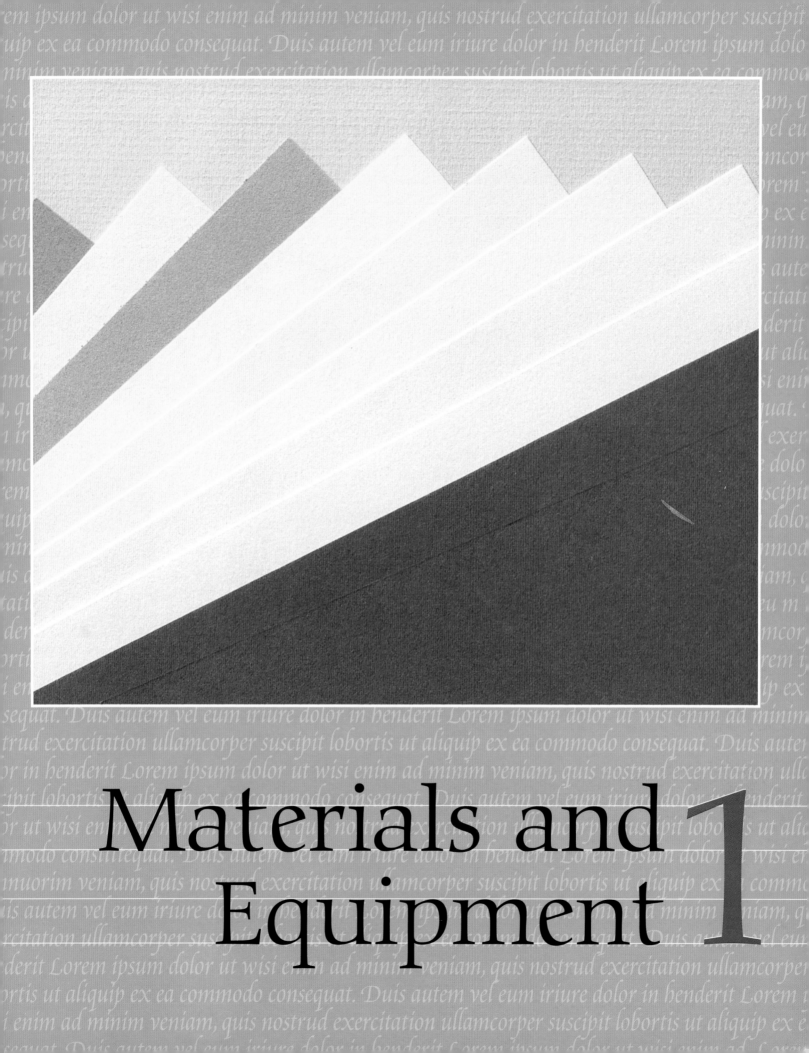

Materials and Equipment 1

Materials and Equipment for the Scribe

Calligraphy, or the study and reproduction of historical lettering styles, as well as the creation of new lettering styles, is today a very popular recreational activity. The array of materials and equipment that is now available to the scribe and illuminator is both very wide and varied in quality. The equipment and materials that you will need at the outset are discussed below.

A selection of metal nibs, holders, and ink reservoirs.

Pens and Nibs

Although metal nibs have been in use since Roman times, early examples were not very satisfactory. Now produced by many different manufacturers, good metal nibs can produce excellent results. It is important that you use proper calligraphy pens and nibs if you want to create really good lettering. Fountain pens may be easy to use, but their nibs are never sharp enough to produce distinctly contrasting thin-and-thick strokes, and it is these that give most calligraphic hands their style and beauty. Nibs come in a wide variety of styles and sizes. For consistency, William Mitchell nibs have been used throughout this book. They are one of the best brands to use. If you buy other brands, you may find that sizes vary. A size 70 for one brand may be another brand's size 0.

A calligraphic pen consists of a nib-holder, a nib, and a small reservoir to hold the ink. The nib is first fitted into the holder (Fig. 1), and the reservoir fitted last (Fig. 2).

After gaining some initial experience with metal nibs, it is well worth trying quills and reed pens in order to widen your understanding of calligraphy and your ability. If you cannot make your own quill pen, you may be able to buy a ready-made one; because demand is small, however, they may be difficult to find. If this is the case, try contacting a local or national lettering society to ask if they know of a supplier or can put you in touch with a scribe who will make pens for you.

A Homemade Quill Pen

Curing a Quill

A quill pen is made from the feather of a large bird, such as a goose or swan. One of the first five flight feathers is used, as these are the largest and strongest (Fig. 3).

A quill needs to be cured before it can be cut. In order to do this, you must first remove the end of the barrel and soak the feather in water for about 12 hours so that the cells expand.

Remove the membrane inside the barrel with a suitable object, such as a small crochet hook or a length of wire, taking care not to scratch the barrel.

When it is free of obstructions, harden the barrel by plunging it into hot sand. Heat the sand (which should be as fine as possible, like the silver sand that is used by potters) in a flat pan and push the quill into the sand so that the barrel is filled. Use a spoon to scoop the sand into the quill if necessary, and leave it in the sand for only a few seconds before removing it to examine it. The opaque, white color of the barrel should have become transparent, and provided that there is no distortion or blistering to the quill from overheating, you can continue to the next stage. If the quill has not been left in the sand for long enough it will be too pliable when it cools, so it will probably be necessary for you to learn by trial and error when the quill has become hard enough to write with, but not so hard as to be brittle when it is cut.

Fig. 1. Attaching the nib to the penholder.

Fig. 3. An untreated quill.

Fig. 2. Fitting the ink reservoir to the nib.

Shake out the sand. While the quill is still hot and slightly pliable, scrape off the membrane from the outside of the barrel with a blunt knife in order to avoid scratching it. Then dip it into cold water and dry it in order to prepare it for cutting (Fig. 4).

Shorten the feather to a length of no more than about 8 to 10" (20 to 25cm) and remove the plume from both sides of the quill. Alternatively, if you prefer to keep a little plume for appearance's sake, you can leave some on the side that will not rest against your hand, although you will find it less cumbersome if you trim this down to about ½" (1cm) in width. All of the barb (the plumage around the top end of the quill) must be removed, as it would otherwise interfere with your hand when writing.

Fig. 4. A cured quill.

Making Your Quill Pen

1 First remove the end of the barrel, then cure as detailed previously.

2 Using a very sharp knife, remove the end of the barrel, cutting along a long, slanting angle.

3 Make a short slit down the length of the quill. Work carefully, and lever the blade gently, until the quill cracks to form the slit.

4 The next cut is a large scoop taken out of the opposite side to the slit, so that the slit is more or less centered in the remaining portion. This cut is quite difficult, as quills are very tough, and you will probably have to experiment on several quills before you produce a good pen.

5 Make a cut on each side of the slit to form the writing edge. Make sure that you match each side so that the slit is central and the pen is of the required width.

6 To make the writing edge clean and sharp, rest the end of the quill on a smooth, hard surface and thin the tip slightly with a forward stroke.

7 Finally, remove a tiny portion from the tip with a downward cut to create a completely straight edge.

Fig. 5. The completed quill pen.

The pen should now be ready (Fig. 5), but dip it in ink and try writing a few strokes to see if it is smooth and well cut. The end of the nib can be recut if it is not correct or after it has become blunt through use.

Ink

The type of ink that you use is very important, as it is difficult to produce good letters with a poor-quality ink. There are many bottled inks on the market, ranging from thin, transparent liquids, which often flow very blotchily from the pen and are likely to fade when exposed to daylight for long periods, to quite acceptable, strong blacks that have the correct consistency. It is worth experimenting with various types of ink so that you get an idea of what is available and which ink is the most suitable for you.

Chinese Ink

The best ink is Chinese ink, which will not fade when exposed to strong sunlight. Although it can be bought in liquid form in bottles, solid sticks of ink that are ground in an ink slate (Fig. 6) produce the highest-quality ink. The sharpness of letter that can be achieved with Chinese ink sticks is infinitely superior to that produced by bottled inks.

Fill the deep end of the slate with enough water to make the quantity of liquid ink that you think you will need. The ink must be freshly ground on the day that you intend to use it because it thickens and goes off if it is kept for too long. It is therefore usually only necessary to grind up a small amount at a time.

Grind the ink stick back and forth along the full length of the slate, taking the water with it until a very strong, black ink is produced. You will need to apply heavy pressure and will probably have to grind the stick for at least 15 minutes.

During the grinding process, keep testing the strength of the ink by painting a little on a sheet of paper to see if it is dark enough when it dries. When you are happy with the appearance of the ink, apply it to the pen with a small brush (Fig. 7).

Fig. 6. Chinese ink stick and slate.

Fig. 7. Applying ink to the nib with a brush.

Papers for calligraphy.

Paper

Good-quality cartridge paper is ideal when you start to practice calligraphy. It is worth buying a pad of I.S.O. A2-sized (596 x 422mm) paper from an art store because the practice lettering that you will begin with will be quite large, and you will therefore need to work on large sheets of paper if you are to fit a reasonable number of lines of lettering onto the page.

Avoid paper that is on the thin side, however, as it will crinkle up when the ink makes it wet. Some papers are also too shiny to take ink very well, and you will either find that your letters are not sharp enough or that the ink sits on the surface of the paper and takes too long to dry. Try to find cartridge paper of about 120gsm (grams per square meter), which should have the right weight and surface quality for your lettering. (See Chapter 9 for different types of paper and a little more on their manufacture.)

Drawing Boards

It is vital that you write on a sloping surface so that the pen meets the paper at the most advantageous angle. When you first take up calligraphy, you can make do with a board—perhaps a piece of fiberboard measuring about 2 by 3' (60 by 90cm) from a D.I.Y. store—resting against a table and on your lap (Fig. 8). As you progress, however, you will find it more convenient to acquire a small drawing board, which you can set up at a fixed angle (Fig. 9). You can buy good drawing boards from well-equipped art stores, and some have a parallel rule attached that can save you a lot of time when ruling up sheets of paper (Fig. 10).

Fixing a few sheets of blotting paper to the surface of the drawing board is an important modification that will enable you to write on a slightly springy surface rather than a hard, flat one. Try to find large sheets of blotting paper that will cover a reasonably large area and fix two sheets to the board with adhesive tape (Fig. 11).

A guard sheet is the next requirement, and this should be as long as your board will allow, as you will need to move the paper underneath it from side to side as you work along each line of text. The positioning of the guard sheet is important: you should find the most comfortable position for writing at your board while also ensuring that your eye level is as shown in Fig. 12. Attach the guard sheet in such a way that the line of lettering that you will be working on appears at the correct level.

As you write, make sure that your hands always rest on the guard sheet and not on the paper that you are writing on. This is very important advice, as no matter how clean you believe your hands to be, they will always deposit small amounts of grease on the paper that they touch. This can have dire consequences for your work because greasy paper will not absorb ink well and you will produce poor-quality letters if you write over any greasy patches.

Fig. 8. Drawing board resting on lap and table.

Fig. 9. Small portable drawing board.

Fig. 10. Large drawing board with parallel rule.

Fig. 11. Add blotting paper to the board.

Fig. 12. Add a guard sheet at the right level for writing height.

The Calligraphic Styles in This Book

Having gathered all of the equipment and materials that you will need, you are ready to proceed. The lettering styles illustrated in this beginner's manual are adaptations of some of the historical examples detailed above that have been modified in the interests of clarity, consistency, and ease of production. Together they constitute an interesting range of hands that are suitable for a wide variety of uses and occasions.

Foundation-hand Lettering 2

Foundation-hand Lettering

When you write formal lettering, one of the first things that you have to consider is the size of your nib in relation to the writing lines that you are going to use. It is always best to start writing between top and bottom guidelines to enable you to make straight, even lines of lettering. Some people like to dispense with the guidelines after a short time, but using them is far more reliable, and it doesn't take much time to draw up sets of penciled guidelines that can be erased later.

Ruling Writing Lines

Writing lines that are five times the width of the nib are appropriate for most lettering styles, and when you begin you should use a fairly large nib, such as the size 1½ William Mitchell nib, which is about ³⁄₃₂″ (2.5mm) in width. You can determine the width of your writing lines by making a series of five small strokes, side by side, with your pen (Fig. 1), which will give you the correct width. You should then rule up a sheet of paper with sets of writing lines. Allow twice the width of the writing lines between each pair of lines to give enough space for the ascending and descending strokes (Fig. 2).

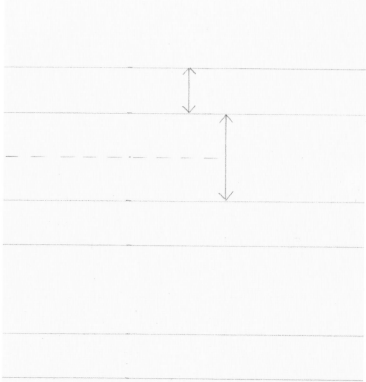

Fig. 1. Five nib-widths are used to determine the height of the writing lines.

Fig. 2. Ruling up a page of writing lines.

Regulating the Ink Flow

Before tackling the foundation-hand alphabet shown in Fig. 3, begin by gaining some experience in using your pen by drawing the various strokes that you can make with it. Dipping the whole nib into the ink tends to be rather messy and leaves a lot of surplus ink outside the space between the nib and reservoir, which is the part of the pen that actually delivers the ink to the edge of nib and thus transfers it to the page. Instead, fill the nib with ink by applying the ink with a small brush and drawing it across the opening between the reservoir and the nib so that the ink fills most of the gap. (see Fig. 7, page 19).

Start by making some diagonal lines following the direction of the pen (Fig. 4), so that the stroke is as broad as the width of the nib. Try to make the ink flow freely and evenly from the whole width of the nib, without leaving any gaps or making any scratches. If you have trouble getting the ink to flow from the pen, you may have positioned the reservoir against the nib too tightly, thereby preventing the ink from flowing through. Reservoirs vary slightly in their manufacture, and some can be a little tight. If you think that this could be the problem, bend back the tip of the reservoir slightly. The side wings can also be adjusted either outward or inward if the reservoir is too tight or too loose.

Another reason why the ink may not be coming out is that the reservoir tip is too far away from the end of the nib. Finally, you may have applied too little ink to the nib so that it is not reaching the writing edge. If you have the reverse problem—too much ink flowing from the pen—then you should either adjust the reservoir so that there is less of a gap between the reservoir and nib or else move the point of the reservoir a little farther from the writing edge.

Fig. 4. Diagonal practice strokes.

Fig. 3. The foundation-hand alphabet.

abcdefghi

jklmnopqr

stuvwxyz

Experimenting With Strokes

1 The angle at which you hold the pen should be about 30° to the paper.

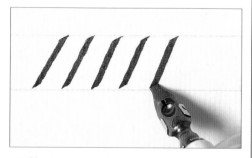

2 When the ink is running smoothly from the pen and your diagonal lines are even, with no jagged edges, try making a zigzag pattern. You are now making the thickest and thinnest lines that the pen can produce, and the nib should be moving from side to side for the thin strokes and in a straight line for the broad strokes. Note that if the correct, 30° angle is maintained, the thin stroke will always be longer than the broad stroke.

3 Next, try some backward-sloping diagonals, which are slightly more difficult to produce. Try to reproduce the same angle and thickness of the strokes shown, as these are written with the pen held at the correct angle.

4 Keeping the pen at 30°, carefully make these strokes and then practice crosses, keeping both parts of the cross well balanced.

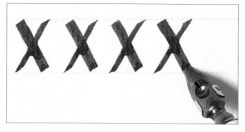

5 Now try some vertical lines, taking care to keep the strokes as upright as possible. If one edge is jagged and the other smooth, you are probably applying too much pressure to one side. Adjust your grip and apply a little less pressure to the smooth edge and a little more to the jagged side, which should solve the problem.

6 Practice some horizontals next. These are a little more difficult than vertical lines, as any error made along the length of the stroke tends to be more noticeable. As you gain experience in the use of your pen, however, any initial unevenness should soon disappear.

7 Curved strokes can give the novice calligrapher a lot of trouble. First, form a series of circles composed of two strokes as shown, trying to keep them as smooth and rounded as possible.

8 To start with, you could draw pencil guidelines and trace the pen around them so that you get used to the feel of the strokes when you are making them correctly. Make sure that the nib does not stray outside the pencil line.

9 Next try strokes that are made up of a combination of round and straight lines.

Foundation-hand Lettering

1 When you are ready, move on to the alphabet, here shown with directional strokes added. This is a simple style called the foundation, or round, hand, because the letters are the foundation of most other styles and are all based on a round, "o" shape. The "o" determines the measurement that governs the width of the other letters.

2 An "n" is exactly the same width as the "o," as are all of the other letters except for the "i" and the "l" (which are narrower because they are composed of only one stroke), and the "m" and "w" (which are in effect double versions of "n" and "v" respectively and are therefore twice the width).

3 The "z" is the only letter for which your pen will have to make one of the strokes at a different angle. When making the central stroke of the "z," turn the pen so that it is horizontal to the page. This produces a thicker stroke, which makes the letter look better than if it were written with the pen held at the normal angle throughout. Work through the letters, making the strokes in the directions shown, and then practice those that haven't worked out very well.

Correct Spacing

Once you begin to write words, you will need to think about the spacing of the letters within them. Spacing takes time to master, but after a while you will automatically find yourself judging it correctly.

The basic requirement is that the letters look in balance with each other and that none are squashed up, or too far apart. In Fig. 5, the letters are unevenly spaced and too far apart; the space between the letters is gradually widening and the letters do not look as though they all belong to the same word. In Fig. 6, the letters are much too close together, giving a cramped appearance that makes the text difficult to read. In Fig. 7, the letters are correctly spaced, with as equal an amount of space as possible between each letter.

It is helpful to look on the letters as groups of three and to make sure that the central one of the three always looks as though it is exactly in the center, and not nearer to either its left- or right-hand neighbor. In Fig. 8, the first two groups of three letters are not evenly spaced. The bottom example is correct.

Fig. 5. The spacing of the letters of this word is too far apart.

Fig. 6. The letters are this time too close together.

Fig. 7. The word correctly spaced.

Fig. 8. The first two groups of three letters are not evenly spaced; the bottom example is correct.

Words that are a combination of similar types, for example, those that consist of rounded letters only, such as those in the word "code" (Fig. 9), or of straight letters only, such as in the word "lilt" (Fig. 10) are much easier to space than those that contain a mixture. Words that combine both rounded and narrow letters, such as "millipede" (Fig. 11), are harder to balance. Here the letters are widely spaced at the beginning and closely spaced at the end.

Try to get into the habit of thinking about the space that you are leaving between each letter and always make it roughly equal. Two straight letters written side by side leave much less space between them than two rounded letters (Fig. 12), so they are moved farther apart to give the appearance of an equal amount of space. With the less regular letters, such as "s," "f," "v," and "t," in which at least one side is neither completely straight nor curved, you will have to try to judge the amount of space needed to give the same effect that would be achieved with more regularly shaped letters.

The spacing between words should be about one letter's width (Fig. 13). If you leave too much space between words, your page of lettering will appear to have too many gaps, or what are called "rivers" of space, running down the page, in other words, the gaps between words will coincide with each other from one line to the next, forming large, blank areas on the page. By contrast, if too little space is left between words, some may look as though they are joined together.

Fig. 9. A word composed mainly of rounded strokes will have the letters almost touching.

Fig. 10. A straight-stroked word will have letters spaced well apart.

fig. 11. A combination of straight and rounded strokes needs proper spacing to look correct.

Fig. 12. Rounded strokes are always much closer together than straight strokes.

Golden slumbers kiss your eyes, Smiles awake you when you rise: sleep, pretty wantons, do not cry, and I will sing a lullaby. Rock them, rock them, lullaby.

Fig. 13. A gap the width of one letter is left between each word.

Practice all sorts of pieces of lettering, paying special attention to any letters that give you particular trouble or to the strokes that you find most difficult to produce. It is wise to spend a lot of time mastering the early learning stages rather than rushing into the more complex styles before you are ready.

Fig. 14 shows the foundation-hand capital, or majuscule, letters. These are written with a letter height that is seven times the width of the nib (Fig. 15), so rule up a page of guidelines for these letters. After writing them in alphabetical order, practice writing groups of similarly shaped letters, such as the rounded letters "C," "D," "G," O," and "Q," moving on to letters that comprise vertical and horizontal strokes only, like "E," "F," "H," and "L," and then to those with diagonal strokes, such as "T," "K," "V," "W," "X," and "Y." Varying the letter order like this will help you to become more familiar with the relationship of each letter to others in the alphabet.

Now write majuscule and minuscule letters together (Fig. 16). Although you can work on this practice piece using guidelines for the five- and seven-nib-width measurements to ensure that you make the capitals the correct height, you would normally only use the height required for the minuscule letters, and would judge the capitals by eye.

In order to write a piece of lettering containing the correct grammar, you will need to insert punctuation marks (Fig. 17) and numerals (Fig. 18). Although the brackets, exclamation point, and question mark are all drawn at capital-letter height, the colon and semicolon look best when they are written with their top marks just below the top minuscule writing line. An ampersand is shown in Fig. 19.

Fig. 14. The foundation-hand capital letters with directional strokes.

Fig. 15. The capital-letter height is seven times the width of the nib.

Fig. 16. Practice the majuscules and minuscules side by side.

Fig. 17. Numerals.

Fig. 18. Punctuation marks.

Fig. 19. An ampersand.

Adding Serifs

The plain letters of the foundation hand are improved and linked with small strokes known as serifs. The various types of serif are constructed as shown in Fig. 20. The full serifed alphabet is shown in Fig. 21, and the serifed capital letters are shown in Fig. 22.

The serif at the top of ascending strokes and at the beginning of most of the capital letters starts with a thin stroke drawn from right to left and then traces an arching curve back to the right again. Now make the upright stroke so that it falls in line with the curving stroke. Do not make the first two strokes too long, or you will leave a small gap in the center of the three strokes and the serif will be too large. These two strokes really only need to be the equivalent of one nib-width to produce the correct-sized serif.

The serifs at the foot of the "f," "p," and "q," as well as many of the feet of the capital letters, are made by taking the pen to the left, just short of the point at which the letter will finish, and then making a horizontal stroke that cuts across the upright without leaving a gap. The other serifs are less complicated, being just a slight curve at the beginning or end of a stroke.

Fig. 21. The foundation-hand alphabet with serifs.

Fig. 20. Types of serif: the first three examples are simple curves completing some of the upright strokes; the following two are composed of two strokes, as shown underneath—a narrow stroke to the left and then the broad stroke completing the serif; the remaining example is a diagonal stroke that finishes with a smooth curve.

Fig. 22. Serifed foundation-hand capitals.

The "m" is a good example of a letter that needs a mixture of slightly different serifs in order to make it look well balanced. The first serif at the beginning of the first vertical is a smaller curve than those that will make up the next two strokes. At the feet of the first and second verticals are small serifs that turn slightly toward the right. The final serif can be a little more pronounced. If this larger serif were used for the first two strokes, it would fill too much of the gap between the vertical strokes and would mar the legibility of the letter.

The cross strokes of the "f," "t," and "z" can just be given a slight turn at either end to add a smooth flow to the letter and to take away the hard, plain look of the unserifed stroke.

It is not necessary—and, indeed, is sometimes even a mistake—to try to join up the letters with too many serifs. Serifs should be simple adornments that give a more pleasing appearance to the text and do not detract from its clarity and legibility. Overdone serifs can really spoil the look of the lettering (Fig. 23) and can also make it difficult to read. The "r" is the letter that is mistreated more than any other in this way (Fig. 24), and when forming it try not to give the foot of the downstroke more than a slight turn, or it will end up looking more like a badly formed "c."

When changing to different lettering sizes, remember to make your writing lines five times the width of the nib. Avoid sizes below the William Mitchell No. 3 nib, which is about $\frac{3}{32}$" (1.25mm) in width, at this stage, because smaller lettering is more difficult. Although it can hide errors, it is better to learn to form the letters correctly from the outset. Fig. 25 illustrates writing lines for lettering drawn with a size 3 and a size 2 Mitchell nib.

Dig. 23. The foot of the "r" is frequently given too large a curve. The correct "r" is on the left.

Fig. 24. Here the correctly written word is shown above.

Fig. 25. Writing lines for nib sizes 2 and 3.

Pen Patterns

Pen patterns are not only good fun to produce, but can also be extremely useful for embellishing small calligraphy projects.

There is no end to the attractive patterns that you can make, and Fig. 26 shows a selection. Practice reproducing them.

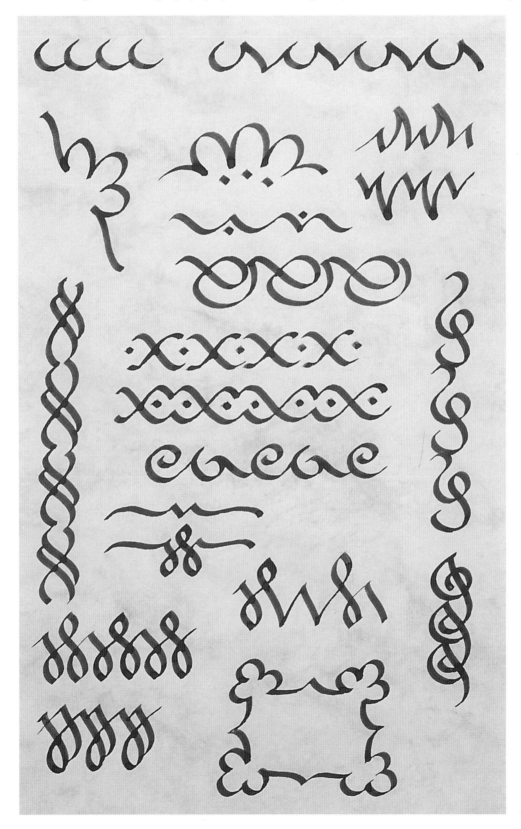

Fig. 26. Pen patterns.

Project

Making Simple Labels

In order to practice and make use of what you have learned so far, you could use the foundation hand to make a few labels for home produce.

Raspberry

1 On your chosen paper, write the main words that will be contained on the label in a large lettering size. Leave plenty of space around the words so that you can trim the label to size.

25th August

2 Write the secondary information in a smaller size on a separate practice sheet. Measure the amount of space that the text takes up and mark this length on the label under the first line.

Raspberry Jam

3 Rule the writing lines for the smaller lettering and mark the width so that it will be centralized beneath the main lettering.

Raspberry Jam

25th August 2000

4 Write the secondary information within the marked space, making sure that it is centered below the first line.

5 Draw a pen pattern around the edge as a little embellishment.

6 You could also add a small line drawing to decorate the label further.

7 Calligraphic line drawings are easy to do: first make a pencil sketch of your subject and then work out the direction of the strokes that will be needed to form a nicely shaped picture. When you have found the best way in which to create the picture, repeat the process on the label.

8 Any fruit shape can be pen-drawn with a little care.

As an alternative to the horizontally laid-out label above, you can follow the same basic steps to create a vertical, or portrait-style label, as shown here.

Compressed
Foundation
Hand

3

Compressed Foundation Hand

The foundation-hand alphabet takes up a great deal of space because all of the letters are quite wide. A more practical width of lettering is achieved by compressing the whole alphabet by the same amount, so that each letter is based on an oval rather than a circle.

In the compressed foundation-hand alphabet (Fig. 1), the strokes forming each letter are produced in exactly the same way as those for the ordinary foundation hand, and the pen angle remains the same, but the width of the letters are reduced so that they all conform to the oval "O" (Fig. 2). The "e" is the only exception, whose second stroke becomes rounded.

A few of the letters have alternative versions (fig.3), which can add more character. The "a" and "g" are based on letters that were used in the alphabets of the early Middle Ages. They can be useful to vary the similarity of some combinations of letters, to add interest to the writing, and also to make it easier to read. Take, for example the word "glade." In Fig. 4, it has been written in compressed foundation hand based on the original letters used for the uncompressed foundation hand. The same word is shown in Fig. 5 using some of the alternative letters, which gives it a little more variety.

abcdefgh
ijklmnop
qrstuvw
xyz

Fig. 1. Compressed foundation-hand minuscules.

Fig. 2. Oval "O" and round "o" to demonstrate compression.

Fig. 3. Alternative versions of some minuscule letters.

glade

Fig. 4. A word written in normal foundation-hand letters.

glade

Fig. 5. The word again using some of the alternative letter forms.

The curved versions of the "v" and "w" are also useful variants. The alternative version of the "z" may be a rather unusually shaped letter, but it removes the necessity for a letter formed with a pen angle that is different to that used for all of the other letters. Some people prefer the diagonally stroked "y" to the other version. The curved "x" is more suited to some work than the diagonally constructed version. Ultimately, however, it is you who has the choice as to which letters you use in particular places. It is worth learning all of the different versions because they will come in useful from time to time.

Compressed Foundation-hand Serifs

The serifs on these letters are the same as for the foundation-hand alphabet, but, because the amount of space between each letter is smaller, remember that it is even more important that they are not overdone. Letters with a curving, final stroke can be linked together easily. If two cross strokes come side by side, they can be joined as shown in Fig. 6.

There are two types of serif that may embellish compressed foundation-hand capital letters. The first set of letters (Fig. 7) is written with the wedge-shaped serifs that we used for the normal, noncompressed version of the foundation hand (see Chapter 2). The second set of letters (Fig. 8) is written with straight, or flag, serifs. These give a stronger and neater impression to the letters and are useful for headings where a bold, clear effect is required, whereas a heading written with letters using the wedge-shaped serifs (Fig. 9) has a little more style.

Fig. 6. Where two cross strokes meet the letters can be joined together.

Fig. 7. Compressed foundation-hand capitals with wedge serifs.

Fig. 8. Straight serifs are added to this alphabet of compressed foundation-hand capitals.

Working With Lettering Sizes

We will now concentrate on the use of different lettering sizes, because it is important to combine them with care. As was described in Chapter 2, foundation-hand lettering should be five times the width of the nib. The chart (Fig. 10) illustrates the nib widths for most of the William Mitchell nib sizes. As you reduce the size of the nib, a greater degree of precision is needed when drawing your writing lines. Although a small inaccuracy will not be very noticeable when the writing lines are ½" (13mm) apart, lines for a size 6 nib that are only ⅛" (2.5mm) apart need to be drawn as accurately as possible. A tiny discrepancy of even a quarter of a millimeter will make quite a difference to the lettering and could make the text look very uneven over three or four lines (Fig. 11). Some of the smaller nibs are not very accurately made, and there is also so little difference between a size 5, 5½, and 6 nib that you will often find, for example, that a nib stamped as a 6 will be wider than a 5. In order to avoid any mistakes, it is always best to make a few sample strokes and to write a few words with the nib that you intend to use and then to check the width for the distance apart of the writing lines before you start.

Fig. 9. A heading written first with wedge serifs, then with straight serifs, to show the different character that each style gives to the text.

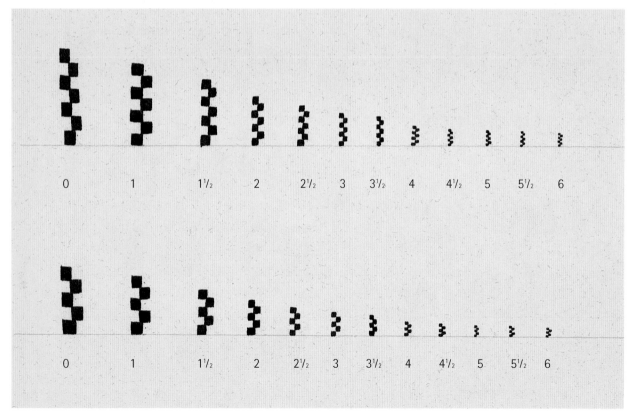

Fig. 10. A chart showing sets of nib widths of all the William Mitchell nib sizes from 0 to 6.

Fig. 11. Writing lines for the small nib sizes must be drawn very accurately as tiny measurement discrepancies, as shown here, can make quite a difference to the lettering size.

Project
Making a Bookplate

When designing a bookplate, remember that the text will look more attractive if it is written in several different sizes.

Choose a combination of nibs, with at least one nib size between them, such as sizes 1½ and 3 (Step 1). Alternatively, try sizes 3 and 4 (Step 2). If you use sizes that are next to each other in the numbering sequence, the difference will not always be great enough to be really noticeable (Step 3), and sometimes, particularly when using the smaller sizes, the text will just look like inaccurately written lettering. For our bookplate project the name will be written with a size 2 nib (Step 4), "This book belongs to" will be written with a size 3, and we will use a size 5 nib for the address.

Now work out the arrangement of the words that will give the best shape to the whole piece of lettering (Step 5). The easiest way in which to do this is to write out all of the words in their respective lettering sizes and then to cut them out and to paste them on a sheet of layout paper in their intended positions. All of the lettering will be centered on this bookplate, so first draw a vertical line down the center of the layout sheet. Then measure and position the cut-out letters centrally down this line.

Step 1. Experimenting with nib sizes 1½ and 3.

Step 2. Experimenting with sizes 3 and 4.

Step 3. Sizes that are too close together will not show enough difference.

Step 4. Choosing the final sizes.

Step 5. Arranging the words to give the best shape to the bookplate.

Making a bookplate (continued)

By looking at this draft version (Step 5), you will see whether the combination of lettering sizes that you have chosen looks right. If you are not sure that it does, try writing some of the words in a different size to see if the balance of the words and the spacing between the lines looks better. Try different combinations of lettering sizes and distances between the lines of text until you find a set of sizes that looks just right. It is well worth taking the trouble to try several sizes, as it is surprising how often you think that the original sizes work quite well together, only to find that altering them slightly produces a much better effect.

For projects such as this, it is not necessary to stick to the writing-line-height formula of twice the letter height between each line of text, which is only necessary for straightforward blocks of lettering that do not involve many small sets of words in different sizes. The size of the bookplate can either be determined by the lettering sizes that you have chosen or you can otherwise work to a specific size and make the lettering fit into it. The bookplate that we will be working on measures 6.3 x 4.7") (16 x 12cm), so the centered arrangement and sizes of lettering illustrated in Step 6 will fit this nicely.

The bookplate can be decorated with a few ornamental flourishes, which you should design in rough and then add to the draft version to make sure that they will all fit properly. The final cut-and-pasted draft is shown in Step 7.

Choose a suitable paper for the bookplate and carefully rule up the guidelines for the writing as accurately as possible. A very sharp HB or F pencil is best for this, as the lines can be rubbed off easily after the text has been written. Do not press too heavily, or you will leave scored impressions of the lines on the paper, even after they have been erased.

Step 6. The complete text in position in the chosen lettering sizes.

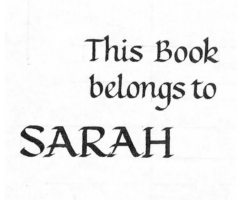

Step 8. Write the text from top to bottom.

Step 7. A border design is added to complete the draft,

Measure and mark the width of each word on the paper so that you can see exactly where you need to start and finish writing each line of lettering. Put in markers, too, to help you to place the pen patterns around the outside correctly.

Write the text from the top to the bottom of the paper, so that your hand is never working over wet lettering (Step 8). Alternatively, if you are writing a larger piece where the lettering on several different areas of the page is of the same size, it can save

time to write all the words of the same size at the same time, but, if you do this, make sure that the ink is completely dry before working on text above words that you have already written. It is easy to be careless when you are ready to start writing the next lettering size and to forget that there may still be wet patches of ink. Serifs and areas of letters where several strokes meet can build up a large amount of ink, which can take quite a while longer to dry than the rest of the lettering.

COMPRESSED FOUNDATION HAND ➥ 39

When you are writing between markers, remember that your lettering will be slightly different from day to day and that a sentence that takes up 4" (10cm) when written on one day may take up much less, or more, space on another, when you may be writing with either more tension or more freedom, depending on your mood. You will also usually find that the first few lines of lettering that you write when you start working will be much more cramped than those written as you are gradually loosening up and writing with more ease and freedom. It is therefore a good idea to warm up with a few practice sentences before working on any text where the spacing is critical.

By looking at your draft, you will see exactly where each line of lettering should start and finish, and, with a little care, you will be able to make sure that the words fall correctly into place. It may be tempting to pencil in all of the words lightly and then to write over the top of them, but this is not a good idea, as you could find yourself trying to make the letters fit the pencil marks and forget about forming them as well as possible. Penciling in words can sometimes be helpful in certain places--especially for the title when you are working on an important document--in order to make sure that you are fitting the words in correctly, but if you get into the habit of doing this your writing style will become too rigid and unspontaneous. If you have trouble fitting words into measured spaces, it is more helpful to remove the text of the draft line by line as you write and to place it above the area that you are about to write on. If you have used adhesive tape to keep the draft lettering in place, it should not mark the paper and should be of the type that can be pulled off easily. Write the words while checking that you are keeping more or less to the spacing on the draft.

This Book
belongs to

SARAH ANN
EAMES

21 Collett Farm Road
Oakenshaw
Durham

Bookplates With Curved Lettering

The first bookplate design that we worked on had a very simple, centered layout. When you want to create something a little different, however, try working on a set of alternative layouts to see if you can find a more interesting arrangement.

1 Here are a series of sketched layout ideas for another bookplate, this time one that is landscape in format rather than portrait (the width is greater than the height). The design will incorporate a small line-drawing illustration of a house, which you could trace from a photograph if necessary. The chosen layout (f) has curved lettering, which is quite easy to write.

2 Use compasses to rule the writing lines. Provided that the curve is not too tight, writing around it presents few problems when using a simple lettering style like this one.

3 Practice writing curved lettering. If the curve is quite tight, you will have to make the letters slightly wider on their outer edges and slightly more compressed on the inner edges. For a project such as this, however, the curve of the letters should be fairly shallow, causing very little distortion to the letters.

4 You will probably need to extend the central measuring line on your draft below the area of the bookplate in order to centralize the curve at the correct point below the paper to give the degree of curve needed for the lettering. When you come to write the actual text, if your paper is not large enough for the compass point to be positioned on it, stick it to a larger sheet and carry down the guideline on to it. The compass point can then be positioned on this

extra sheet to make your guidelines accurately, with the added advantage that no pinhole will be left on the bookplate. A full-circle design is also illustrated, with filler patterns drawn on either side of the words to fill the spaces. The central writing line on this piece curves quite tightly, so that the capital letters have had to be carefully written to fit between the writing lines correctly. The overall effect is satisfactory, however, and the design works well.

Project
Making Bookmarks

Bookmarks are another simple way of using calligraphy. They are fairly straightforward to produce. The writing lines need to be carefully positioned for the various lettering sizes.

Simple Horizontal Bookmark

This shows a simple, vertical bookmark with pen-pattern borders.

1 The small lettering around the outside of the design is quite close to the edge of the card. Because it can be difficult to write to the edges of small pieces of card--they tend to move easily and will not always lie completely flat--write this piece of lettering on a larger sheet of card on which the outside edges of the bookplate have been marked and then cut the card to size when the text is finished.

2 This shows the completed bookmark.

Bookmark With Curved Lettering Between Parallel Lines

1 Here curved lettering is written between writing lines that have been carefully measured. Make the first line in any shape.

2 Then measure out the line height at small intervals along its length. Next, join these intervals to give as smooth a curve as possible at the correct distance to the first.

3 Add flourishes to the ascender and descender strokes to fill the remaining space.

Bookmark With Nonparallel Lines

1 This bookmark uses writing lines that are not parallel to each other, which gives a different effect. You will need to spend time working on the draft in order to achieve writing lines that run smoothly and make attractively spaced words.

2 Trace the writing lines and transfer them to the card.

Bookmark Using Masking Fluid

2 Write the letters with masking fluid using a large nib, paint over any areas that are too thin with a small brush to give a thick covering.

1 Layout for a bookmark using masking fluid. Use it in a pen, just like ordinary ink--it flows quite well and can make good letters. Small nib sizes are best avoided, however, as the letters will not be very accurate.

3 Work through the lettering, then add the flourishes at the end.

3 Paint a color wash of gouache over the letters with a large brush.

4 When you are sure the paint is completely dry, remove the masking fluid with an eraser.

Using a Ruling Pen

Ruling pens and compasses are useful for all sorts of purposes in calligraphy, and can be used to create some outer decoration.

Ruling pens and compasses are used in many ways.

Using a paintbrush, apply ink or paint to the gap between the two ends of the pen. Experiment on a scrap piece of paper until you have become accustomed to putting the correct amount of ink into the pen.

Draw the pen along the edge of a beveled rule (Fig. 12), making sure that the ink does not come into contact with the rule itself. If it does, it will smudge when you remove the rule. Remember, too, that if you overload the pen with ink, the ink will gush out and make a large blob, while too little ink will result either in patchy lines or in no ink reaching the points.

The pen can be adjusted to draw a thick or thin line, but take care not to make the line too thick, or you will increase the risk of producing a blob of ink on the page. Ruling compasses, which work in exactly the same way, enable you to draw perfect circles with ease.

Fig. 12. The ruling pen is drawn along the beveled edge of a rule to prevent the paint from touching the rule.

Bookmark With Ruled Border

1 Layout for a bookmark with a ruled border.

2 Write the lettering, then rule in the lines.

Italic Lettering 4

Italic Lettering

We will now move on to italic lettering, which is basically the same as the compressed foundation hand, but with a slope to the letters of about 10° from the vertical as illustrated in Fig. 1.

When writing in the italic hand, the most important thing is to keep a constant degree of slope throughout the piece of lettering, as words written at different angles look very untidy. As with the previous two alphabets that we worked on, keep the pen at an angle of 30° to the writing lines. If you have difficulty keeping the letters at the same forward angle of slope throughout your lettering, draw in a few diagonal guidelines at intervals across the page to help you until you have become used to the correct angle. The letters are formed as shown in Fig. 2.

This alphabet is a formal italic, which is more regular and rounded than the sharper, and more angular, cursive italic (which will be the subject of the next chapter). The rounded "a," "e," "g," and "y" are shown here, but the alternative versions used with the compressed foundation hand can also be used with italic.

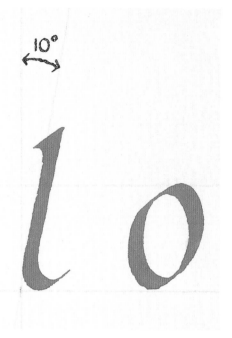

Fig.1. Italic letters are written with a slope about 10° from vertical.

Working With Color

You may need a selection of different colors when you are planning and writing a piece of lettering, such as a menu. Writing with colored inks can be different from using black ink because the colors are usually of varying consistencies. There are a great many bottled colored inks on the market, and many are sold as calligraphy ink. As with black ink, the quality varies enormously, but most are generally rather thin and transparent and flow too quickly from the nib for fine letters to be produced satisfactorily. It is nevertheless worth experimenting with types of colored ink, and if you are satisfied that you can produce similar results to black lettering, the ink should be of good quality.

It is also easy to write with paint. Gouache is a water-based paint that works very well when used in a pen. It comes in small tubes in a vast range of colors and should be mixed with water in a small palette or suitable container (Fig. 3). The

Fig. 2. Formal italic alphabet.

Fig. 3. Gouache paints, mixing palette, and mixing brush.

consistency required for calligraphy is like very thin cream. The paint should be a good, opaque color, but not too thick to clog the pen. When writing in several different colors, you will find that they vary slightly in consistency. Some colors are quite grainy—the browns tend to be like this—while greens can be difficult to make opaque without the use of a slightly thicker consistency than is required for most other colors. Always practice a few words in any newly mixed color before working on your final piece of lettering to make sure that the consistency is correct. When working with paint, it is a good idea occasionally to rinse and wipe the nib to make sure that the paint hasn't dried under the reservoir or on the outside edge.

The range of gouache colors is large, because when different gouache colors are mixed together they lose some of their brilliance. You should therefore avoid mixing two or more colors together and should instead choose a single color from the range. All colors have their advantages and disadvantages, so your choice will usually be a compromise when selecting the best one for your work. Some of the most useful colors are listed on the following page.

Gouache Paint

Burned umber is a soft, donkey-brown color. It is quite dark when used straight from the tube and therefore usually needs a little white added to it. Because this is another color that tends to fade quickly, however, keep the shade as deep as possible when mixing.

Scarlet lake is the best red by far: it is a lovely, strong, bright color, and when it is mixed with water its opacity and consistency are very good. Because it tends to smudge when you are erasing any writing lines across which it has been written, when mixing it with water it is a good idea to add a drop or two of gum arabic to make sure that the paint remains firmly attached to the page.

Spectrum yellow is a bright, deep yellow, whose strength should be sufficient if you are writing on a pale-colored surface. If necessary, you could add white to it to make it more opaque, but if you do so try to use as little as possible because white has a heavier consistency than most other colors and the paint will not flow smoothly from your pen if you use too much. (Writing with white paint is not recommended.)

Purple lake is an attractive color to choose when you need a purple color--Parma violet is another good choice. Of the two, purple lake--a reddish-purple color--does not fade in the light as quickly, whereas Parma violet, which is on the blue side of the color spectrum, is more opaque.

Permanent green middle is a good, medium-colored green (there are also dark and light versions of this color). Although greens are inclined to fade when they are exposed to sunlight, this color lasts better than most of the others. It tends to be transparent when it is mixed to the correct consistency, in which case you could add a little white to it, but remember to be sparing with the white because the paler the shade of green, the more prone to fading it becomes.

Ultramarine is a strong, bright blue. Although its color is extremely vibrant when it is used straight from the tube, it tends to be a little transparent when mixed to the correct consistency. If this happens, add a little permanent white to give it greater opacity.

Rose Tyrian is a shocking-pink color that you may find useful on occasions.

Chinese ink sticks are also available in various colors (Fig. 4), although these are not as widely available as bottled inks and gouache paints. Grind colored ink sticks with water in an ink slate (Fig. 5) in the same way as black ink sticks until you have obtained the correct consistency and depth of color.

Fig. 5. Colored ink sticks are ground on an ink slate in the same way as a black ink stick.

Fig.4. Colored Chinese ink sticks.

Making a Menu and Place Cards

The menu should be no larger than I.S.O. A4 (298 x 211mm) size, which is a standard paper size from which printed copies can easily be made. You will need three different sizes of nib: one for the title, one for the name of each course, and one for the details of the food.

When designing the menu, begin by roughly drawing out the wording in the order and general shape in which you intend it to appear (Step 1). This will give you an idea of the spacing required for the quantity of lettering to be included.

Work out if your chosen sizes will fit the overall dimensions that you have decided upon for the menu. If you are using a size 4 nib for the body of the text, the line height will be $^5/_{32}$" (4mm), with $^{11}/_{32}$" (8mm) between each set of writing lines. Determine if this will enable you to fit all of your text into the size of paper that you intend to use by measuring out the writing lines down the

length of the draft sheet. You will find that a size 4 nib will produce lettering that takes up too much space to fit the required menu size comfortably. You should therefore try a size 5 nib for the small-sized lettering.

Enough of a margin needs to be left around the edges to make a reasonable border, as well as for the holly-leaf decoration in the corners (Step 2). Using the line-height guide (which was explained in the previous chapter), try to guess the nib sizes that may be suitable for the other two sizes of lettering that you will be using.

Start by working on the smallest lettering and write out one of the sections in rough to see how it will look (Step 3).

Now work out which size will be best for

the course headings (Step 4). The first lettering is too large, so use the smaller size (Step 5). Make a draft of all of the lettering for the courses to check that everything will fit on your paper.

Work out the lettering size for the title (Step 6). It is worth writing the title in several sizes and then cutting them out and trying each in turn. Now add a border (Step 7).

Once you have decided on and drafted all of the lettering to size, rule up your paper or card with the writing lines. Some very attractive papers are available in large sheets or pads of different colors, and a selection is shown in Step 8. If you want a really special paper, you could go to a specialist paper store that has sample books for you to look through and choose from the hundreds of colors, textures, and weights of paper available. (For more on paper and card, see Chapter 9).

Step 1. Initial sketch of menu contents.

Step 2. To ascertain whether your chosen nib sizes will fit the page, mark off the writing lines down the length of a sheet. The column of marks to the left allow for a size 4 nib for the small text, but this leaves too little room for the border. The column to the right is measured for a size 5 nib, and this will leave plenty of room for the border.

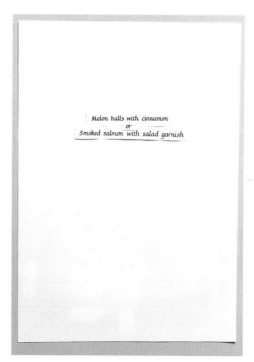

Step 3. Write out and position the small text roughly in place on the layout sheet.

Main Course

Main Course

Step 4. Two sizes of course heading are then experimented with.

Step 5. The chosen size positioned on the draft.

Step 6. Try the title in a choice of sizes.

Step 7. Add the border to complete the draft.

Step 8. A selection of papers and cards: Constellation Pearl card in satin and shantung patterns; Conqueror laid card in green, pink, and blue; Parchmarque paper in white and four colors; Canford card, three colors from an extensive range; Ingres pastel paper in a pad of three colors.

Making a Menu and Place Cards (Continued)

An attractive, fairly thick, but lightly textured, paper has been chosen for the menu (Step 9). In the closeup photograph (Step 10), you can see the grain of the paper, which is quite pronounced. If you choose a paper with a characteristic like this, make sure that you buy some extra sheets for experimenting on. When using a smaller-sized nib in particular, take care that it does not catch on any raised fibers in the paper. Most papers do not present much of a problem, but it is very annoying if you catch your nib on an uneven area and send a spattering of ink across the paper. Although errors can be removed from most good-quality papers (see page 84–87), prevention is better than cure.

Measure and rule your guidelines and marking points onto your chosen paper. Now you are ready to write your menu card (Step 11).

Write the title in scarlet lake gouache, a lovely, bright red that will really enliven your work.

Permanent green middle gouache will be used for the course headings, so make sure that you have mixed it to the correct consistency so that the writing will not be transparent. Using a guard sheet, write in all of the course headings, taking care that you don't touch the writing surface with your hands.

Add the smaller details in black ink.

Gold paint gives a very good effect for details, and a little has been used in the corner decoration and lines between the courses. Winsor and Newton manufacture a gold-colored gouache, with a rich gold color similar to real gold. It needs to have quite a thick consistency when it is applied in order to cover the paper well without looking patchy. There are other good gold-substitute paints available, too, such as that produced by Pelikan, but these can be quite difficult to find.

When you have finished, carefully erase the writing lines, taking extra care around the red lettering if you have used gouache. Use a very soft eraser so that it does not mark the paper.

Matching place cards can also be designed. These are very simple to produce.

First, write a draft set of the guests' names to help you to measure and correctly center each name on its card. Then add a small holly-leaf decoration. Finally, draw in a border with a ruling pen to echo the menu's design.

Step 9. The chosen paper is cream-colored Parchmarque card; the surface is quite textured, but smooth enough for lettering.

MENU

To Start

Melon balls with cinnamon

or

Smoked salmon with salad garnish

Main Course

Duckling a l'orange or Roast Lamb with mint sauce

Step 10. The texture of the paper is clearly visible.

Step 11. Writing your menu.

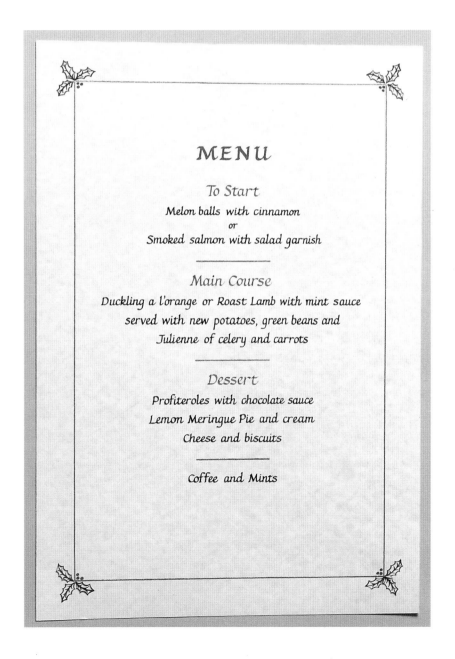

MENU

To Start
Melon balls with cinnamon
or
Smoked salmon with salad garnish

———————

Main Course
Duckling a l'orange or Roast Lamb with mint sauce
served with new potatoes, green beans and
Julienne of celery and carrots

———————

Dessert
Profiteroles with chocolate sauce
Lemon Meringue Pie and cream
Cheese and biscuits

———————

Coffee and Mints

Designing a Certificate

1 Cut-and-paste draft lettering to determine the arrangement of the landscape layout.

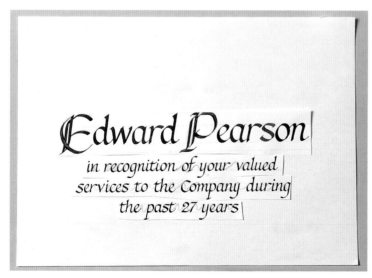

2 Begin the draft with the main title, then centralize the smaller text below.

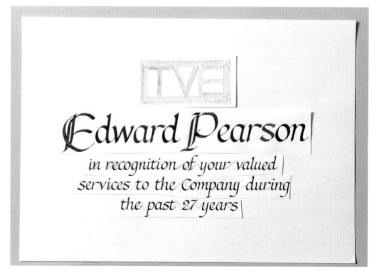

3 Adjustments can be made to the lettering sizes to determine the best combination. Next, the logo, dates, and "To" are arranged in positions that give the best overall balance.

To TVE 1972–1999

Edward Pearson

*in recognition of your valued
services to the Company during
the past 27 years*

4 This shows the completed draft.

*Company during
t 27 years*

5 The paper chosen for this certificate has a mottled, marble effect and is called Marlmarque. The writing lines are lightly ruled to avoid making indentations in the paper. Add marking points for the start and finish of each line of text. Now you are ready to write your certificate.

Designing a Certificate (Continued)

A size 1 nib is used for writing the main name and a size 2½ for the three lines of text below. The other words are written with a size 1½ nib. The large initial letters in the main name and "To" are large, italic letters written with double pen strokes for the downstroke of each letter. The same size 1 nib is used, even though the letter height exceeds the usual seven nib-widths for capital letters; this is because double strokes make the letters larger and extend them below the bottom writing line. They have each been adapted from other lettering styles to add a little more interest to the design, which, for an I.S.O. A4-sized certificate, contains quite a small amount of text. (Double-stroke letters are covered in more detail in the next chapter.)

The positions of the two large, gold letters can be ascertained by using the draft as a guide. These are written first.

The black text is written next, so that it falls correctly into place after the gold initials.

"To" and the dates are now written, and then finally the lines of text at the bottom.After the text has been completed, the logo is sketched or traced into position. The background colors are now painted. The green and gold lettering and logo are painted in gouache colors.

The outline of the logo is drawn, using a ruling pen for precision.

Finally, the writing lines are removed, care being taken not to smudge the lettering.

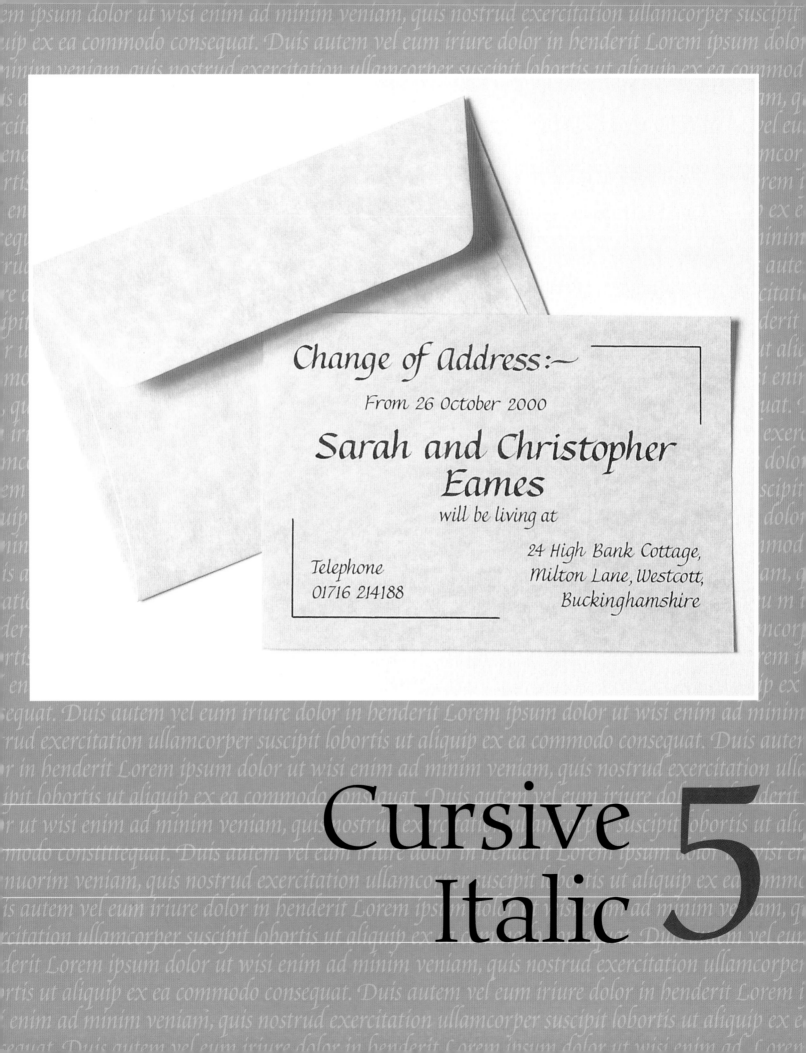

Change of Address:~

From 26 October 2000

Sarah and Christopher Eames

will be living at

24 High Bank Cottage,
Milton Lane, Westcott,
Buckinghamshire

Telephone
01716 214188

Cursive Italic 5

Cursive Italic

Cursive italic, in which there is more of a contrast between the thick and thin strokes, is a more stylish version of the italic hand than formal italic. Cursive italic can be adapted to form a handwriting style that is quick enough to be practical, yet still retains characteristics of the more formal calligraphy styles.

Fig 1. Connecting strokes for cursive-italic letters.

Before attempting the whole alphabet, practice the strokes illustrated in Fig. 1. These are the two connecting strokes that make this style markedly different from formal italic (compare the two types in Fig. 2). Cursive-italic lettering can also be written with more continuous stokes than formal italic.

The whole alphabet is illustrated in Fig. 3. Notice that the tops of some of the rounded letters have been flattened out slightly (Fig. 4). The serifs, especially the tops of the ascending strokes, are much sparer than those used with formal-italic letters. Most are just a subtle rounding-off of the stroke at its beginning and end (Fig. 5), which both aids the speed of writing and makes the style simpler and clearer. The "f" is usually given a long tail with a bottom stroke to match the "g," "j," and "y." When a more decorative style is required, this lettering style really lends itself to extravagant flourishes and elongated serifs. (These will be dealt with later in the chapter.)

A set of simple, unadorned capitals that match cursive-italic minuscules are illustrated in Fig. 6. Like the minuscules, they have been constructed with minimal serifs and fewer lifts of the pen. They are quite plain, modern-looking letters, which have a very distinctive feeling of flow and movement. These have been used in the piece pictured in Fig. 7, which is the text of a passage from Shakespeare's *Romeo and Juliet*, giving the speeches of each in turn in two alternating colors. (The text is written on blue Conqueror card, which has a laid surface. This card is smooth enough for calligraphy that is written with a fairly small nib, and it also takes ink very well.) Fig. 8 shows a few alternative versions of the cursive-italic capitals.

Fig. 2. Letters "a" and "n" in cursive italic and formal italic. Cursive is on the left.

Fig. 3. The cursive-italic alphabet.

a c g *l*

Fig. 4. Rounded letters are written with flattened-out top strokes.

Fig. 5. Minimal serifs are used for cursive-italic letters.

ABCDEFGH
IJKLMNOP
QRSTUVWX
YZ

Fig. 6. Simple cursive-italic capitals.

> If I profane with my unworthiest hand
> This holy shrine, the gentle sin is this;
> My lips, two blushing pilgrims, ready stand
> To smooth that rough touch with a tender kiss.
>   Good pilgrim, you do wrong your hand too much,
> Which mannerly devotion shows in this;
> For saints have hands that pilgrims' hands do touch,
> And palm to palm is holy palmers' kiss.
>   Have not saints lips, and holy palmers too?
>   Ay, pilgrim, lips that they must use in prayer.
>   O! then, dear saint, let lips do what hands do;
> They pray, grant thou, lest faith turn to despair.
>   Saints do not move, though grant for prayers' sake.
>   Then move not, while my prayers' effect I take.
> Thus from my lips, by thine, my sin is purg'd.
>   Then have my lips the sin that they have took.
>   Sin from my lips? O trespass sweetly urg'd!
> Give me my sin again.
>
>   *From Romeo and Juliet by W. Shakespeare*

Fig. 7. An excerpt from *Romeo and Juliet* in cursive-italic lettering.

Fig. 8. Some alternative cursive-italic capitals.

Writing Change-of-address Cards

When you are designing a piece of text, you will not always want to center all of the lettering, and when you are planning a piece whose lettering is off-center, it is important to achieve a good balance of lettering and spacing across the whole page. This is illustrated by the following simple project--a change-of-address card--whose text is shown in draft form in Step 1. The nib sizes used for this piece were a size 3 for the main name, a size 4 for the top line of lettering, and a size 5 for the remaining words.

Sketch out a few alternative layouts to see which looks the most attractive (Step 2).

The first example, the straightforward, centralized layout, is neat, but rather uninteresting. The second example shows a gradual shifting of the lines of text across the page, from top left to bottom right, with the telephone number fitted into the empty bottom left-hand corner. Vertical layouts are not very practical for this type of card, as the names of people and places need to be split between too many lines to allow ease of reading. The best choice for this piece of lettering is example b, which has a landscape layout, with the text gradually stepping down from left to right.

Make a draft of all of the lettering (Step 3), using the appropriate nib sizes. Cut out the words and arrange them on a layout sheet, making alterations as necessary until you are satisfied with your complete draft.

Measure and rule your guidelines and marking points onto your chosen card. You are now ready to write your change of address card (Step 4).

Using a ruling pen, add linear fillers to the two empty corners to balance up the design. The finished card, which was written on peach-colored Parchmarque card, has a matching envelope.

Step 1. Text required for a change-of-address card.

Step 2. A set of alternative sketched layouts for the change-of-address text.

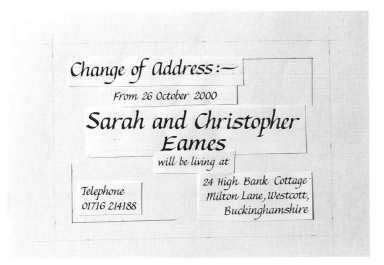

Step 3. Cut and paste the text into the chosen layout.

Step 4. Lettering your change-of-address card.

From
26 October 2000
Sarah and
Christopher Eames
Change of Address
will be living at
24 High Bank Cottage
Milton Lane, Westcott,
Buckinghamshire
Tel. 01716
214188

Fig. 9. A diagonally arranged change-of-address card on mauve Canford card.

Fig. 9 shows an alternative design for a change-of-address card. The text has been written diagonally, in black ink and mauve gouache, across lilac-colored Canford card (Canford is sold in a range of colors and is available from many art stores).

Flags and Flourishes

Cursive italic can be sharpened to an even greater extent than the examples shown so far, and Fig. 10 shows letters that have very acute curves to the beginning and end of their strokes, as well as thin, hairline strokes connecting the main changes of pen direction. Note that the tails of the letter "p" have been given a backward serif to indicate an increased sense of movement (Fig. 11).

sharpened letters

Fig. 10. Cursive-italic letters sharpened further to give greater contrast between strokes.

As was previously mentioned, cursive letters lend themselves to exaggerated serifs and flourishes. Fig. 12 shows some of the minuscule letters to which it is particularly easy to give this treatment. They are all letters with an ascending or descending stroke that can be given a "flag" serif to accentuate the forward-flowing movement of the lettering style. Combinations of letters can also be linked to good effect (Fig. 13).

Capital letters written in this style are even more adaptable to flourishes, and the alphabet shown in Fig. 14 illustrates the letters with several variations of flourished strokes.

sharpened

Fig. 11. The serif on the leter "p" flows into the down stroke from behind.

Fig. 13. Combinations of letters can be linked together.

Fig. 14. Flourished italic capitals.

6 d f h p

Fig. 12. Flag serifs on ascenders and descenders.

A A B B C D E F
F G G H H I J
K K L M M N
N O P Q Q R R S
T U V V W W
X X Y Y Z Z

Hairline serifs are sometimes added to the extremities of cursive-italic letters to give an added touch of finesse. You need to be fairly adept with your pen to create a good effect with these, however. A very slight flick of the pen is all that is needed (Fig. 15), so that only the left corner of the nib remains briefly in contact with the paper. Note that this type of stroke should be a casual embellishment and not a studied addition (Fig. 16) to the letters because this destroys their charm and spontaneity.

Monograms

You can design a monogram by building up a capital letter with a series of flourishes. The best way in which to go about designing it is first to work it out in pencil. Remember that it takes a while to achieve a good design that has smooth, flowing curves and an interesting shape.

Try to keep most of the flourishes on the outside of the letter, which will make it easier to see the letter itself—the design's *raison d'être*, after all. The "A" in Step 1 has a simple series of loops at its top and bottom, which curve around and back over themselves several times before ending in a final curl.

Make sure that the design is balanced by ruling a dividing line vertically through the center of the letter and keeping a balance of pattern on both sides (Step 2). Now trace your design onto your card (Step 3).

Step 1. An "A" monogram.

Step 2. A dividing line is used on the pencil draft to help balance the design.

Fig. 15. Hairline serifs.

Fig. 16. Overworked serifs.

Step 3. The letter is traced onto the card, giving pencil guidelines to follow when making the flourishes.

Once you are happy with your pencil outline, work out the best way of making the pen strokes to achieve the best effect. Keep the pen angle the same as when writing ordinary letters, so that you produce the same contrasting thick-and-thin strokes. If you find that some of the strokes are a little difficult to form, such as the long, thin, diagonal strokes from right to left (Step 4), adjust the design to limit these as much as possible.

Step 4. Take care with the thin, diagonal strokes, which are the most difficult to produce.

You cannot make the whole flourish with a single pen stroke because a metal nib does not work properly when it is dragged backward for the thin strokes. Each part of the flourish should therefore be a separate stroke (Step 5), which join up perfectly around the curves (Step 6).

The letter can either be made double-stroked to give an interesting effect (Step 7) or consist of a combination of single and double strokes, which makes a letter look larger and bolder as its limbs appear wider, being composed as they are of two strokes and the space in between. The "N" shown in Fig. 17 has double strokes for each of the three strokes forming the actual letter and curving terminations at each corner. Fig. 18 shows a double-stroked "H" monogram.

With more complex designs, you may find that when you draw in some of the thicker pen strokes the design can look a little congested in the areas where several strokes cross over each other (Fig. 19). Such strokes can also close up some of the gaps, thereby completely spoiling the design. These areas therefore need to be adjusted so that the strokes are more evenly spaced on the final design (Fig. 20).

Two letters give even more scope for creating scrollwork with which to link the letters (Fig. 21 and Fig. 22). Use a smooth piece of paper or card for this work to be sure that you will be able to make the strokes in a flowing, graceful manner. After you have worked out the design, either go straight ahead and try writing it freehand or use a pencil outline as a guide.

Step 5. Each part of the flourish should be a separate stroke.

Step 6. The separate strokes should join up perfectly.

Fig. 17. An "N" monogram composed of double strokes.

Fig. 18. A double-stroke "H" monogram.

Fig. 19. This "Q" monogram has areas where the cross strokes are too congested.

Fig. 20. The redesigned "Q" monogram now has better-spaced crossing strokes.

Fig. 21. "LC" monogram.

Fig. 22. "PG" monogram, with double-stroke letters.

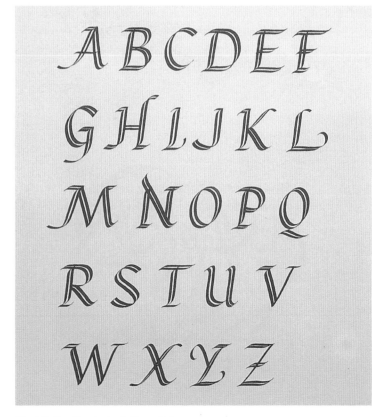

Fig. 23. An alphabet of upright double-stroke capitals.

Fig. 24. Double-stroke italic capitals.

Double-stroke Letters

Double-stroke letters can be useful for titles or the initial letters of verses, and an alphabet consisting of double-stroke capitals is shown in Fig. 23. An alphabet of double-stroke italic capitals is shown in Fig. 24. Although these letters were written with a size 3 nib to a height of 1¼" (32mm), you have a lot of latitude when constructing letters in this manner. For example, the same-sized nib also made the letters illustrated in Fig. 25, showing that it is possible to work to a given size and space in order to fill it to best advantage.

A few of the letters have been broken down in Fig. 26, and the order in which the strokes were made has been given to help you to master their construction. You will need to practice some of the letters a great deal before you write them, in order to get used to the correct order of stroke construction that is needed to form the best shape. As you can see, double-stroke letters work equally well when they are either upright or have a cursive, forward slant.

When constructing the letters, ensure that where combinations of strokes meet you work them into each other carefully so that you do not end up with an unattractive jumble of lines that meet incorrectly. The letter "A" is one of the more difficult to construct as a double-stroke letter because the lines cross in several places.

For letters with curved strokes, such as "B," "C," "D," and so on, the outer curve should be written first, so that the shape is correctly established before the inner curve is added. Where the horizontal strokes running across the bottom of a letter meet the curved strokes, the outer curved stroke should join the top horizontal stroke and the inner curved stroke the bottom horizontal stroke (Fig. 27).

Fig. 25. The same-sized nib wrote these three different-sized double-stroke letters.

Many of the letters, such as "V" and "W," look better if one or more of the strokes are left as a single stroke. Others, such as "L" and "Y," benefit from the addition of a balancing stroke to maintain an even distribution of weight across the letter.

Fig. 28 is a piece of lettering in which double-stroke initials begin each of the verses, as well as the title. The title letters have been given a more decorative treatment by means of a few additional flourishes. The letter "H," in particular, lends itself to this sort of treatment.

With regard to the layout of this piece, note that the verses have been offset to the left and right down the page, thereby giving greater width to the whole design. A piece such as this, which has five verses with quite short lines, makes rather a long, narrow column running down the page if the verses are written directly beneath each other. This design spaces the larger initials within the block of text better. The sets of four lines of each verse were given the same treatment by means of stepping alternate lines in and out of each other at the same interval.

Fig. 26. The order in which the strokes are made needs to be worked out and followed carefully.

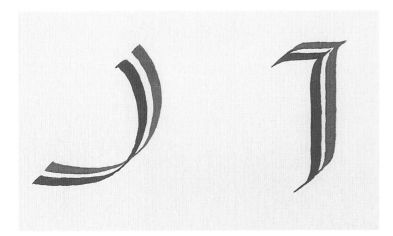

Fig. 27. Take care to join up inner and outer strokes correctly.

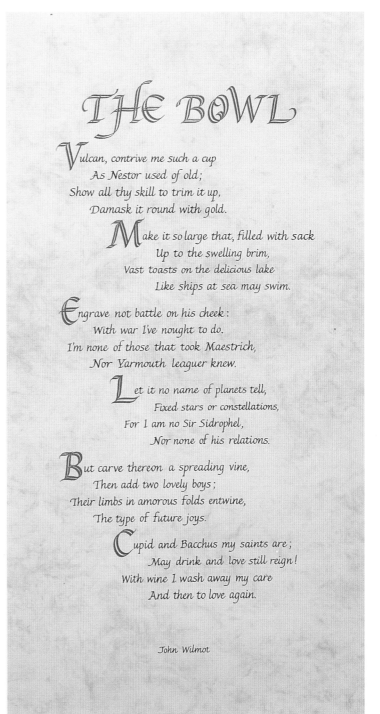

THE BOWL

Vulcan, contrive me such a cup
As Nestor used of old;
Show all thy skill to trim it up,
Damask it round with gold.

Make it so large that, filled with sack
Up to the swelling brim,
Vast toasts on the delicious lake
Like ships at sea may swim.

Engrave not battle on his cheek:
With war I've nought to do.
I'm none of those that took Maestrich,
Nor Yarmouth leaguer knew.

Let it no name of planets tell,
Fixed stars or constellations,
For I am no Sir Sidrophel,
Nor none of his relations.

But carve thereon a spreading vine,
Then add two lovely boys;
Their limbs in amorous folds entwine,
The type of future joys.

Cupid and Bacchus my saints are;
May drink and love still reign!
With wine I wash away my care
And then to love again.

John Wilmot

Fig. 28. Text with double-stroke capitals.

Double-stroke letters are also useful for large-sized lettering because the double-width stroke forms a letter that is a lot larger than the single-stroke capital when written with a nib. Making double-stroke letters can also enable you to avoid working with very wide nibs, which are sometimes a little awkward to use or may produce inaccurate lettering if the nib is not sharp enough or if it contains too much ink. If you do not want your double-stroke letters to be too large in comparison to the rest of the single-stroked lettering, however, you will need to use a smaller-sized nib.

You can buy pens with points of varying distances and thicknesses (Fig. 29) that make a double stroke for you. The points are usually quite fine, with the result that the letters that they produce are lightweight, with a transparent appearance (Fig. 30). The example shown was written with a nib-size 50 Mitchell "Scroll Writer." A music pen is also available (Fig. 31), which has five points for drawing musical staves; of the five strokes produced, the top and bottom strokes are slightly broader than the central three. Such pens are fun to experiment with, and you can also achieve some interesting effects with them.

Fig. 29. A double-stroke nib.

Fig. 30. Letters produced by a double-stroke nib.

Fig. 31. A five-line music-stave nib.

Elswood Horticultural Society

SPRING

FETE

and Plant Sale

Saturday 15th May 2000

ELSWOOD VILLAGE HALL

from 1pm – 5pm

Admission £1

Gardening Advice   Books   Cake Stall   Tombolla   Refreshments   Craftwork   Paintings   Animal welfare

Using Capitals 6

Using Capitals

Calligraphy is often needed when writing posters, and we will deal with some poster projects in this chapter. We will tackle layout further and also look more closely at large capital letters, in particular Roman capitals, which were originally quite complex in construction, but can today be adapted to form a simpler, modern style.

Roman Capitals

Fig. 1 displays the alphabet of Roman capital letters, while in Fig. 2 they are grouped into their different widths. From these examples we can see that the "O" is completely circular, the "C", "D," "G," and "Q" are also based on a circle, while the "H," "M," "N," and "W" are the full width of the "O."

Fig. 3 shows the narrow letters, which are just over half the width of the "O." Note the economical use of fairly small, straight serifs. The remaining letters are shown in Fig. 4. In the Roman-capital-letter alphabet, many of the letters that began with a serif in the alphabets that we previously learned instead begin with a continuous, straight, vertical stroke downward (Fig. 5), which is followed by a top stroke that forms the serifed portion. The letters "B," "D," "E," "F," "P," and "R" have received this treatment, which is similar to the straight–serifed alphabet (Fig. 8, page 35), but has slightly different proportions to the letters. The difference between Roman and foundation-hand capitals is that the foundation-hand letters are all of fairly equal proportions, allowing for their different shapes, whereas the Roman letters are either distinctly wide or narrow, depending on their letter shape.

The Romans were very precise and mathematical in the lettering techniques that they used for forming inscriptions on monuments, and they constructed their letter shapes so that they balanced well. Although the same degree of precision cannot be attained with pen-written lettering, the general proportions can be adapted to good effect for work in which clarity and impact are important, such as posters.

Fig. 1. Roman capital letters.

Fig. 2. Wide letters.

Fig. 3. Narrow letters.

Fig. 4. The remaining letters, which fall between the two widths.

Fig. 5. Strokes forming the top part of many of the Roman capitals.

Posters

We will incorporate text advertising a spring fête (Step 1) into a poster. The main points of the text that should be emphasized are the name of the event and its date, time, and place; the remaining details are less important.

Because the paper sizes used by printers are usually the I.S.O. "A" sizes, if you are planning to have the poster reproduced, it is best to plan your design according to whichever of these "A" sizes suits your requirements best. The full series of sizes that you are likely to use is: A0 (1192 x 844mm), A1 (844 x 596mm), A2 (596 x 422mm), A3 (422 x 298mm), A4 (298 x 211mm), and A5 (211 x 149mm), each ascending size being double the previous one. A4 is the size that is commonly used for office stationery, while A3 is typically the size of the posters that you frequently see fixed to trees and village noticeboards, and our poster will be A3 size.

When creating your artwork, you can either make it the size that you want it to be printed or scale it up slightly and then ask the printers to reduce it to the correct size for the poster. The advantage of having your original artwork reduced in size for printing is that it will sharpen up the lettering and minimize any minor inaccuracies. One disadvantage, however, is that because lettering for posters often needs to be quite large, making it even larger can give you the problem of finding large enough nibs with which to write the work. Never make your original artwork smaller than you intend the printed version to be, however, because when it is enlarged any minor inaccuracies will be magnified, while lines that appeared quite even in the original version will look as though they have uneven edges.

In order to scale your work up or down in size, simply mark the dimensions that you require the finished item to be on a sheet of layout paper (Step 2) and then draw a diagonal line from corner to corner, extending the line outside the required dimensions for an enlargement. Work in the opposite way when reducing. Draw a vertical line upward from any point along the bottom line—for example, if you want an enlargement of 50%, draw the line from a distance half as far again from the original width. Where the vertical line meets the diagonal line, draw a horizontal line to the left-hand edge. The proportions of the new rectangle will now be precisely correct for an enlargement of 50%.

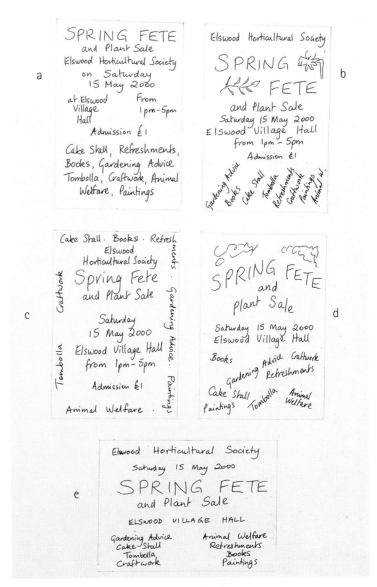

Step 1. Five sketches for a poster for a spring fête.

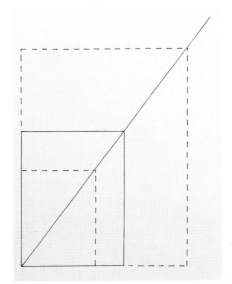

Step 2. Scaling the paper size up or down.

Working on Poster Layouts and Designs

Of the five preliminary sketches for the layout of the spring-fête poster, layout b, has been chosen as having the best balance and clarity. It has a bold title and a little floral decoration in the spaces to the right and left of the words, and although the diagonally written words in the bottom portion are easy to read, they do not detract from the more important lettering.

Taking the alternative layouts in turn, the layout of option a is a fairly straightforward arrangement, with nothing particularly eye-catching about the design. In addition, the main title, which runs across the top of the page, has less impact than the same words in the other four arrangements. Running on the list of words in the bottom portion in a continuous row, separated only by commas, makes the text a little more difficult to read quickly and is also a rather static design. Choice c is made quite interesting by writing the smaller details around the edge of the poster, but this reduces the space available in the center for the more important text, which would have greater impact if it were larger. Although layout d is an attractive design, its different lettering angles make it a little too fussy. As is demonstrated by example e, a landscape arrangement is not very practical for posters because the majority of the places in which they will be displayed, such as in store windows or on trees and noticeboards, suit a portrait-shaped poster better.

Step 3 shows the cut-and-pasted draft of the text for the preferred layout. The capital letters that make up the words "SPRING FETE" can be given special treatment, and we will use Roman capitals written with a size 3 automatic pen (see page 74). The remainder of the description of the event, along with its date, place, and time, will be written in compressed foundation hand. The title across the top of the poster will also be in compressed foundation hand, and you should make sure that the lettering is of a size that will enable you to fit all of the words on one line. The venue will be given prominence by means of widely spaced Roman capitals, while the remaining details at the bottom of the poster will be written in italic to introduce a little variety. This means that three different lettering styles will be used for the text, and because any more would create a discordant appearance, this is about the maximum number of styles that you should include on one page.

When ruling the writing lines for the diagonal words at the bottom of the poster, make sure that you keep them parallel by turning the page and marking the measurements accurately. If you do not have a parallel ruler, draw the first diagonal at the correct angle and mark off the other lines from this, using three sets of points per line (Step 4) to ensure that they are accurate.

Measure and rule your guidelines and marking points onto your chosen paper and write your poster, following the draft (Step 5).

Step 3. The cut-and-pasted poster draft.

Step 4. Using three measured points to draw diagonal writing lines.

Step 5. Writing the poster.

Step 6. The finished poster.

Alternative Poster

Another set of information for a poster advertising a craft fair has been cut and pasted into position in Step 1. The main title is in italic letters written with an automatic pen (Step 2). Roman letters spell out the venue details and the contents list at the base of the page, while two further sizes of italic have been used for the rest of the text. Remember that small calligraphic fillers are useful for breaking up areas of text, and two very simple, linear motifs have been added to this layout to separate some of the central details. The finished poster pictured (Step 3) has text written in black ink on a bright-lemon-yellow card.

Printers usually offer a good range of colors for posters, but if you want a specific type of paper—perhaps with a mottled effect or a laid texture—you can buy your own from a specialist paper store and ask the printers to use that. However, remember that this is only worth doing if you can hang some of the posters where they will be closely scrutinized. Because most posters will usually only be seen from a distance, using a subtly textured or colored type of paper may be a wasted effort.

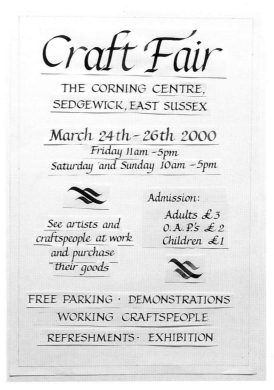

Step 1. A cut-and-pasted draft for a poster advertising a craft fair.

Step 2. Lettering the poster.

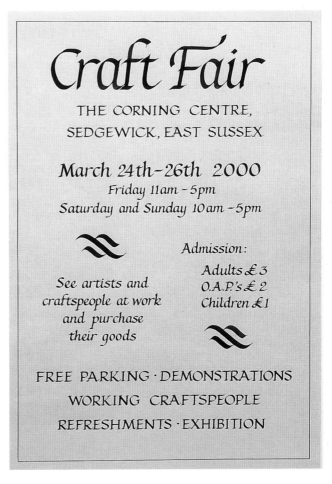

Step 3. The finished poster.

Poster and Automatic Nibs

For posters, your lettering sizes will probably have to be larger than usual. The William Mitchell nibs that we have been using up to this point go up to a size 0, which makes a stroke that is just over ⅛" (about 3mm) in width, giving a capital-letter height of ⅞" (about 22mm). If you need to produce letters that are larger than this, you could buy a set of poster nibs (Fig. 7), to each of which a large reservoir is attached that holds the increased amount of ink required. You will have to

Fig. 7. Poster nibs.

take care not to overfill the nib, otherwise you will produce blotchy letters and lose the fine lines that are integral to good calligraphic letters. Hiro Leonardt also makes large-sized nibs (Fig. 8), whose reservoirs are positioned above, rather than below, the nib.

Automatic pens (Fig. 9) are excellent for poster-writing, as

Fig. 8. Hiro Leonardt nib.

they are not only sold in very large sizes, but are also easy to use. Their construction includes two angled pieces of metal with touching edges and a series of small slits along one edge that allows the ink to flow better. When working, make sure that the slitted edge is facing away from the page as you write. Although these pens can be dipped into a container of ink, some of their nibs are so large that they have to be filled with a large, well-loaded brush in order to transfer the ink to the whole of the inside edge. (Be extremely careful when you are moving a fully loaded pen from the inkpot to the paper, although once you are holding the pen at the correct angle to the paper and are ready to write, the danger of spilling the ink is past.)

Fig. 9. Automatic pens.

For the craft-fair poster, a number 3 automatic pen was used to write the title. The width of the stroke is nearly ¼" (about 5mm), giving a letter height of about 1" (25mm). The pen decoration was also written with this pen size.

Writing Signs

If you need to work on a very large scale—if you are making a sign, for example—you have two options regarding pens. Firstly, you could make your own pen.

Making Your Own Poster Pen

1 Here we are using a piece of absorbent material cut with a thin edge. The example shown is a piece of cardboard with a small piece of cotton fabric wrapped around the end that is held in place with staples. It is rigid enough to provide a good edge for the lettering and the cloth absorbs enough ink or paint to make the letters.

2 Mix plenty of ink, because when you are making large letters with a very absorbent nib you will get through it very quickly. Refill the nib frequently in order to avoid a dry brush effect.

3 The sign illustrated was written with this type of writing instrument on an interesting, Japanese paper flecked with tiny, metallic squares. The width of the stroke made is just over 1½" (40mm), so letters of just under 8" (200mm) could be written if necessary. This lettering has a height of nearly 7" (175mm).

Project
Making a Cork Nib

2 Then cut across it to remove a portion.

3 Now scallop off the back edge to leave a thin edge of cork.

1 Cork is another good nib-forming material, and a cork from a wine bottle should be long enough for your purposes. You will need a very sharp knife to cut it into shape and remember to take care when cutting because the cork is quite rubbery and can be difficult to cut. The completed cork nib is quite robust, however. Start by making a straight cut downward, into the cork.

4 The shape so far should look as shown here.

5 Scallop off side portions to make the end of the nib the required width, then shave it down until it is less than $1/16$" (about 1mm) thick, so that it will give accuracy to your letters.

6 If the writing edge is not straight, make a downward cut along its length. Your nib can also be reshaped if it becomes blunt. (This is more or less the same method that was used to make reed pens centuries ago.)

The "Raffle" sign (Fig. 10) shown was written with a cork nib about ¾" (19mm) wide, and the letters were written between guidelines about 3½" (90mm) high. You will need a small tray of ink, so that when you are dipping the cork pen into it the ink is transferred along the whole of the writing edge. Although you will have to dip the pen into the tray many times—and should be careful to avoid ink drips—the letters can be formed fairly easily, with a good degree of accuracy.

Your second option is to make compound letters, which are letters whose individual strokes are composed with more than one thickness of nib. Compound letters are often drawn first and then written and painted. Being very clear and well-defined, Roman characters—which are often constructed as compound letters—are eminently suitable for signs. The lettering for the sign pictured in Fig. 11 was first drawn and then outlined with a size 3 automatic pen before finally being filled in with a paintbrush. This procedure gives a nice calligraphic quality to the letters, as well as retaining the accuracy that can be lost when using large, home-made nibs.

Waterproof Signs

If a waterproof sign is required, use acrylic paint, which is mixed with water but becomes waterproof when it is dry. Although the paint is quite thick, which means that the letters will not have the accuracy of gouache-painted characters, a little crudeness is not very noticeable in large-scale letters. Indeed, the overall effect can be very good (Fig. 12). If the sign needs to be freestanding, use mount board, which is sold in large sheets and in a wide range of colors by most art stores and picture-framers.

Fig. 10. This sign was written with a cork nib.

Fig.11. "CAKES" sign in Roman letters.

Fig. 12. A sign made using waterproof acrylic paint.

Automatic Pens

The "TEA ROOM" sign pictured in Fig. 13 was written with a size 6 automatic pen. Even a pen of this size can produce lines that are very accurate. Unfortunately, the amount of ink that is required for each stroke often necessitates refilling the nib halfway down a stroke, so take care that you rejoin the line very accurately.

When you are using slightly transparent inks or paints, a dark-and-light effect can be produced where a stroke has been stopped and restarted, as can be seen on the letters in Fig. 14. In order to reduce the chance of this happening, it is therefore best to stick to either black or very dark colors.

The size 6 automatic pen makes a stroke about ¾" (19mm) wide, so capital letters written at the usual seven nib-widths would be about 5¼" (133mm) high. Remember that letters on posters tend to look better when they are a little squatter than normal-sized lettering. Six nib-widths have therefore been used for this sign, resulting in better-proportioned letters.

The "EXIT" sign in Fig. 15 was written with a size 6a automatic pen, whose nib is about 1" (25mm)wide. The lettering is nearly 6" (150mm) high, which makes for quite a large sign —this one measures 8¼ x 29½" (210 x 750mm). Although the quality of the letter edges starts to diminish with this size of nib, it is not enough to mar the lettering when viewed from the intended distance.

Fig. 13. "TEA ROOM" sign made using a size 6 automatic pen.

Fig. 14. Transparent letters produced with ink that is too thin.

Fig. 15. "EXIT" sign using a size 6a automatic pen.

St. Stephens, Barwich

Monies contributed and collected out of the parish of St. Stephens in Barwich, towards the releife of our afflicted bretherin in Ireland:~

Mr. Samuel Dickson	ten shillings	
Mr. Thos Cobb	seven shillings	six pence
Mrs. Newman	ten shillings	
Daniel Hopper	five shillings	
Goodwife Hargreave	one shillinge	
Edward Morris	three shillings	
Richard Morris	sixe shillings	
John Williamson	eight shillings	
Joseph Austin	three shillings	
Nic: Eckleston	foure shillings	
Will: Potterton	one shillinge	
James Shaw	two shillings	sixe pence
Goodwife Shaw	one shillinge	
Edm. Carter	one shillinge	
John Carter	one shillinge	
Sarah Carter		six pence
Hen: Cunningham	one shillinge	
John Walker		eight pence
Margaret Thomson		sixe pence
William Smith		six pence
Walter Palmer		six pence
Edw: Salter		six pence
Jeremiah Whitlock		six pence

Sharpened Gothic Lettering 7

Sharpened Gothic Lettering

We will now move on to a more decorative style: sharpened Gothic lettering. The Gothic styles are angular, and the well-known blackletter hand––which is the most angular of all––will be covered in the next chapter.

The sharpened Gothic style represents a halfway stage between the lettering styles that we have covered so far and the black-letter hand. The alphabet—which is very attractive—is based on the pointed "o" (Fig. 1), which has sharp points where the top and bottom strokes meet. The two halves of the letter should appear to be reversed images of each other, so that the curve of the stroke is exactly the same on both sides.

The full alphabet is shown in Fig. 2. The same angle of curve that is used for the "o" is required to form all of the rounded letters, so practice writing "a," "b," "d," "e," and "o" together so that you learn the correct formation of these strokes. Although the "q" contains a rounded stroke next to an upright, the small stroke that joins the first curved stroke to the upright begins as though it were another fully curved stroke. The "p" contains an arching crossbar that links the upright to the curved stroke. The same type of stroke is used to form the letter "s" (Fig. 3), in which the middle diagonal stroke is the same as in an ordinary "s," but then the top and bottom arching strokes are added. The "c" and "r" use this arching stroke for their top strokes, too, and it also appears at the bottom of the "j."

Pay particular attention the tails of the "g" and "y" (Fig. 4), in which a very narrow, diagonal stroke connects the body of the letter to the final downstroke and the tail. Because it has a diagonally ascending stroke, you will also have to concentrate on the "d" (Fig. 5)—it takes some practice to make the top curve correctly so that it joins up with the bottom part of the letter in the correct place. A strategy that should help you to form the first part of the letter correctly is to imagine that you are just going to write an "o" and then to add the extra top portion as an afterthought.

Most of the letters that are normally written with more than one vertical stroke—the "h," "m," "n," "v," and "w"—have a curved stroke following the first vertical. Practice these letters together to get used to the stroke formation.

The serifs of this alphabet are not very pronounced, those on all of the vertical strokes being no more than a slight curve

Fig. 1. The pointed "o" on which sharpened Gothic is based.

Fig. 2. The sharpened Gothic alphabet.

to the right at the start of the letter. The feet of the "p" and "q" also have small, horizontal serifs.

The capitals for this hand are illustrated in Fig. 6. The letters that differ the most from those that we have already used are the "E" and "T," which are formed with a curved stroke for the main body of the letter. Although the top stroke of the "E" is arched, the "T" has a straight, horizontal stroke. Note that the "N" has a curving second stroke.

Fig. 3. The construction of letters with arching crossbars.

Fig. 4 The construction of "g" and "y."

Fig. 6. Sharpened Gothic capitals.

Fig. 5. The construction of a "d."

Project
Historical Documents

Its historical appearance makes this style appropriate for any document that you want to look old, and the transcription of the historical document illustrated in Step 1 is written in this hand. With the more elaborate lettering styles, it is especially important to think carefully when combining different styles and sizes because some do not go together very well.

An attractive, vellum-effect paper called Elephanthide, which comes in two thicknesses and two colors, was chosen for this work. A sheet of paper that has a relatively heavy weight is generally better for calligraphic work than a lighter alternative because it is less inclined to buckle when wet and you will also be able to remove any mistakes more successfully.

The document lists the contributors to a special collection for a church that was made in 1641. Red, sharpened Gothic letters have been used for the title, which should be the most prominent piece of text. In common with most Gothic styles, because the capital letters of this hand are quite difficult to read when grouped together, a large lettering size in a combination of upper- and lower-case letters is preferable to a title that consists solely of capitals. This lettering was written with a size 1 Mitchell nib.

The description of the collection was written in sharpened Gothic with a size 3 Mitchell nib. The smaller details that appear in two columns running down the page use compressed foundation hand. (Any very small lettering on a document is always best written in one of the more legible styles, like this one.) The nib size that was used was a 4.

Measure and rule guidelines and marking points onto your chosen paper and write out the document (Step 2).

St. Stephens, Barwich

Monies contributed and collected out of the parish of St. Stephens in Barwich, towards the releife of our afflicted bretherin in Ireland:–

Mr. Samuel Dickson	ten shillings	
Mr. Thos Cobb	seven shillings	six pence
Mrs. Newman	ten shillings	
Daniel Hopper	five shillings	
Goodwife Hargreave	one shillinge	
Edward Morris	three shillings	
Richard Morris	sixe shillings	
John Williamson	eight shillings	
Joseph Austin	three shillings	
Nic: Eckleston	foure shillings	
Will: Potterton	one shillinge	
James Shaw	two shillings	sixe pence
Goodwife Shaw	one shillinge	
Edm. Carter	one shillinge	
John Carter	one shillinge	
Sarah Carter		six pence
Hen: Cunningham	one shillinge	
John Walker		eight pence
Margaret Thomson		sixe pence
William Smith		six pence
Walter Palmer		six pence
Edw: Salter		six pence
Jeremiah Whitlock		six pence

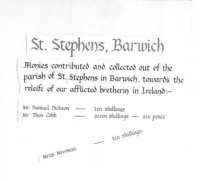

Step 1. The required text. Three lettering sizes are needed.

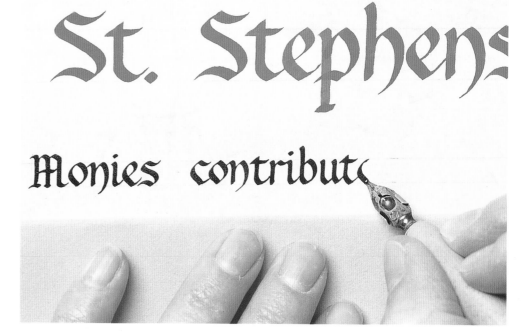

Step 2. Write out the text, then remove the writing lines.

Completing the Document

The document was finished with a simple tying ribbon, which you can attach as follows. First, fold over the bottom edge of the paper so that its thickness has doubled or tripled. Next, make two slits through all of the layers of paper, using a sharp knife and a ruler (Step 1). The slits should be parallel to each other, about ³/₄" (2cm) apart and a fraction wider than the width of your chosen ribbon. Remember not to position the slits either too close together or too near the bottom of the page, or else the paper may tear when the ribbon is tied.

Step 1. Cut two slits, the width of the ribbon, through each layer.

Thread the ribbon through the slits (Step 2). If the paper is reasonably stout and the slits are wide enough, you should be able to pull the ribbon gently through the slits without damaging the paper, leaving the ribbon firmly attached. Now trim the ends of the ribbon to make a neat finish (Step 3).

The document can now be rolled up from the top and the ends of the ribbon tied around the center (Step 4).

Step 2. Thread the ribbon through the slits.

Step 3. Neaten the frayed ribbon ends if necessary.

Step 4. The scroll can be rolled and tied for presentation.

Removing Mistakes

Because it is so easy to be distracted and then to write an incorrect letter, you will often make mistakes when you are writing large amounts of lettering. If you are using a good-quality paper, you should be able to remove the error and then rewrite the correct version on the same spot, leaving little or no evidence of a correction having been made.

Several tools are useful for removing errors (Fig. 7). We will cover this subject in some detail because the more advanced your calligraphic skills become, the more complex the pieces that you are working on will also become. If you don't remove any errors that you make, you will have to abandon, and then rewrite, an intricate piece of work on which you have already spent a lot of time.

Fig. 7. Error-removing tools. From left to right, soft brush, pencil eraser, bone folder, scalpel, burnisher, gum sandarac powder and pumice powder.

Project
Removing Errors With an Eraser

A pencil eraser with a hard, white, rubber core is the most useful tool for removing errors because you can rub away at a very small surface area without greatly disturbing the surrounding letters or paper. The eraser will usually be quite hard, so it is advisable to practice using it on a spare piece of paper to see how hard you need to rub in order to remove the incorrect area. Note that although it is easy to scuff the paper-- especially a soft pape, like cartridge paper-- you should be able to rub quite hard at thicker, better-quality papers without causing any irreparable damage. When you have removed all of the incorrect area (Step 1), carefully brush away any rubber particles and paper dust that may be lying on the paper.

You will now need to smooth the surface of the paper with a bone folder (a burnisher can also be used). This is a small, flat piece of bone, with either two rounded ends or one pointed and one rounded end, which is mainly used in bookbinding to flatten and sharply crease folded pages. Because there will be a variety of occasions on which you may need a bone folder, you will find it a cheap and useful tool, and you can buy one from a specialist art or paper store. If your bone folder has a round and a pointed end, use the round end gently to rub and press the loosened paper surface down (Step 2). By experimenting on a scrap of paper, you will be able to ascertain how much pressure you can apply before the fibers become too crushed and an unwanted indentation is made on the surface.

Try writing over the repaired area to see whether the new letters can be written successfully or whether you are going to have problems with either a surface that has become too roughened or with spreading ink. If the surface is still too rough, burnish it a little more. If the ink spreads too much, try carefully rubbing a little pumice powder and gum sandarac into the surface, which should hold the ink in place (Step 3). Pumice powder and gum sandarac, as well as a mixture of the two, called "pounce," are available to buy. Although these powders are principally made for preparing the surface of vellum skins for writing, they also can be used on paper. Lightly dust the prepared area with a little of the powder and then gently rub it in with a clean cloth, using a light, circular action so that you do not give any marked direction to the fibers. Finally, dust away any excess powder so that it does not clog your pen. Now carefully write in the correct letters (Step 4).

You should not be able to see any marks on the paper--the word should look as if no mistake was ever made (Step 5).

Step 1. Remove the incorrect letters with a pencil eraser.

Step 2. Use a burnisher or bone folder to smooth the roughened surface flat again.

Step 3. If necessary, rub in a little "pounce" to improve the surface.

Step 4. Write the correct letters in carefully.

Step 5. Remove the writing lines.

Project

Removing Errors With a Knife

Another method of removing errors is to scrape away the incorrect areas with a very sharp scalpel or craft knife. (These are available from most art stores and you can buy spare blades cheaply.) Remember that a very light touch is needed when doing this, in order to avoid damaging the writing surface (Step 1). Because some vellum is very thick and quite a lot of the surface skin can therefore be removed before any damage is caused, this method is particularly useful when you are working on vellum. When you have removed all of the erroneous area, burnish the vellum flat so that it can be successfully written over again (Step 2). Now write in the correct letters (Step 3).

If your paper is quite thin and you can see that the ink has worked its way through the whole thickness of the paper when you turn it over and examine the reverse side,

there is no point in trying to remove the letter. If you do, you will be left with a hole. In this case, you have no choice but to start again. Although you could try to paint out the incorrect areas with a similarly colored paint to the paper, this is invariably a very unsightly way of making corrections because they are likely to be obvious afterward, especially since any new letters written over painted areas are usually of poor quality (this is because ink will spread on most painted surfaces). The best way in which to avoid the problem is to use a good-quality paper, which will have been manufactured with this sort of treatment in mind.

The colorings or patterns of some of the more decorative papers are sometimes only on the surface, so that when you remove the top layer you will be left with a different color--usually white--underneath. When

this happens, you will have to try to restore the lost pigment.

First, gently rub a little pigment that matches the color of the paper onto the discolored area before dusting away the residue. Although powdered pigments are available, it is much easier to use a good-quality, colored pencil of the correct shade (Step 4), such as one of the Derwent pencils. Derwent pencils, which are sold by many art stores, are available in a very wide range of colors, including quite a large selection of the light beiges and browns that are useful for pale-cream-colored papers. They are soft pencils, and if you use one very lightly and then rub the colored-in area with a soft cloth (Step 5) to disperse the pigment farther, you should be able to disguise the alteration to the extent that it can only be seen on very close examination.

Step 1. Use a sharp scalpal or craft knife to remove the incorrect letters.

Step 2. Smooth the surface flat again with a burnisher.

Step 3. Write the correct letters.

Step 4. If, as in the example, the paper pigment has been removed, after erasing the writing lines use a colored pencil of the correct shade to replace the pigment, then use a tissue to work the pigment into the paper.

Step 5. The corrected word.

Project
Designing a Family Tree

A handwritten family tree can make a very attractive document to hang on the wall. If you have researched your family history, you could make a chart that contains the names of as many current family members and ancestors as you like. You could also include some interesting pictures, maybe of places that have a family connection or of the professions of some of the people named.

Step 1 shows the text of a simple, four-generation family tree, which should be within the scope of most people whose grandparents can provide the necessary information.

Begin by sketching your information in the form of a rough, drop-line chart (Step 2), which will enable you to see what form the general shape and layout will take. Drop-line charts are created by placing the names of a married couple side by side, with an equal (=) sign between them denoting their marriage. The husband's name is usually placed on the left and the wife's on the right, but you do not have to adhere rigidly to this convention if the other way round suits your layout better. The marriage's date and place are written underneath, usually in a smaller lettering size.

Draw a vertical line descending from the equal sign. Next, arrange the names of the children of the marriage horizontally, in order of age, from the eldest on the left to the youngest on the right (Step 3).

Because there is no equal sign if the children belong to a single-parent family, the line proceeds downward from the center of the information given about the parent (Step 4). The names of unmarried partners can be written with a plus (+) sign between the pair of names to differentiate them from married couples, and then a line descending from the plus sign can be drawn (Step 5). With the ever-growing complexity of family relationships and the possibility of various

combinations of biological, step-, and adoptive parents, family trees will inevitably become increasingly difficult to organize clearly. However, the main thing to remember is that your principal objective is to create an attractive and informative chart, and you should therefore use whichever means suits you best for conveying the information. Provided that you make sure that it is clearly legible and unambiguous, any layout is acceptable.

Write out the name of each person in a large lettering size (a size 4 nib has been used in the example), and then inscribe their biographical details underneath with a smaller nib, such as the size 5 used here (Step 6). Because they are only needed as a guide for the final piece, it does not matter if the smaller details are not perfectly centered beneath the name.

Rule up a large sheet of layout paper with the correct number of lines for the generations that will appear on your chart (Step 7).

Family Tree of Andrew and Sarah Grey

Andrew Grey, born 15.2 1936, married 24.9. 1965 Catherine Parker, born 12.1.1938, parents of:
1) Michael Grey, born 4.4.1967, married 5.8.1995 Sarah Cornish, born 15.9.1970
2) Steven Grey, born 3.11.1969
3)Cara Elizabeth Grey, born 27.2.1971

John Michael Grey, born 1.12.1909, married 7.5.1931, Elizabeth Walters, born 17.9.1910, parents of:
1) William Grey, born 9.6.1932, married 6.9.1959 Jane Daniels, born 2.11.1936, they have one child - Ann Lisa Grey, born 4.12.1963
2)Roger Grey, born 7.4.1934
3)Andrew Grey

Henry Grey, born 17.9.1883, married 5.8. 1905 Mary Carter, born 6.7.1884, parents of:
1) Sidney Grey, born 27.8.1907
2)John Michael Grey

James Parker, born 2.7.1913, married 16.9.1937 Mary Latham, born 24.5.1913, parents of:
1)Catherine Parker
2)Edith Parker, born 2.11.1939, married 14.5.1963 John Williams, born 1.4.1938
3) John Parker, born 5.3.1942

James Parker, born 29.5.1880, married 2.7.1906 Louisa Bellman, born 6.9.1883, parents of:
1)James Parker
2) Doreen Parker, born 18.2.1915
3)Edward Parker, born 6.8.1918

Step 1. The text of a four-generation genealogy.

Step 2. Sketch a rough draft of the genealogy in a drop-line format.

Step 3. The formation of a drop-line genealogy.

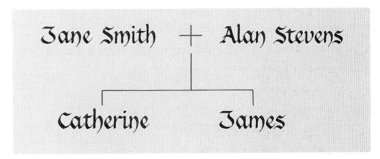

Step 4. For a single parent, take the line down centrally below the name of the parent.

Step 5. A plus sign can be used to indicate unmarried partners.

Andrew Grey
b. 15. 2. 1936
m. 24. 9. 1965

Catherine Parker
b. 12. 1. 1938

Step 6. Write out each name on layout paper and add the biographical details underneath, trying to centralize the information.

Step 7. Rule the required number of generation lines on a layout sheet.

Designing a Family Tree (Continued)

Now cut out and paste the names onto the sheet and arrange them to form the best layout (Step 8) by placing each name in its correct order on the page just beneath the relevant generation line. Leaving a gap of about ½" (1cm) below the generation lines will be sufficient and will enable them to be used to construct the connecting lines.

When the names are all in their correct positions, link the names of husbands and wives with equal signs. Then draw a pencil line downward from each set of parents to the generation line beneath (Step 9). If the children's names are not immediately below their parents', the line should stop just short --about ¼" (5mm)--of the line below, so that a connecting line can be drawn to the left or right to meet up with the line associated with the correct set of children.

Using the horizontal generation lines, link the names of each group of siblings with a heavier pencil line by drawing a line above each group of children, from the first to the last name, and then penciling in a small-- about ¼" (5mm)--line from the horizontal line to the name of each child (Step 10). If the line descending from the parents has not yet been connected to the horizontal line, draw in the relevant section. Do this throughout the chart until the whole network of family groups has been correctly linked.

Add a title in a suitable lettering size, which you can center at the top of the sheet. The completed draft is shown in Step 11. Write out the text (Step 12), working through the larger lettering first. Rule the writing lines carefully and use your draft lettering to determine the spacing of each name by measuring and marking the length of each set of words on the page.

Work through the smaller lettering in the same way. You may not need to mark the length required for all of the smaller details, as the name above can often be used as a guide by noting at which point the smaller details start and finish in relation to the letters above them. Now add the title. Rule in the lines that make up the connecting framework, drawing them in with a ruling pen and a contrasting color of gouache paint. Remove the writing lines.

Step 8. Add the drafted names to the layout sheet in the correct sequence.

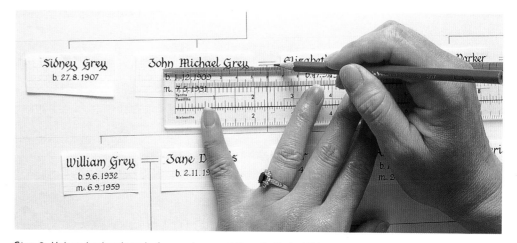

Step 9. Link up husbands and wives and connect them to their children.

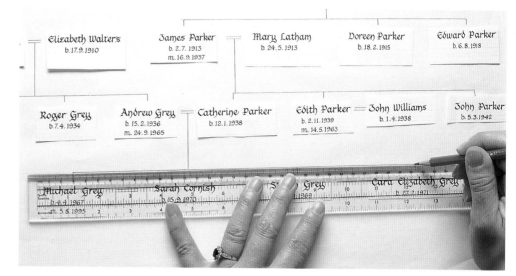

Step 10. Rule in the lines connecting the groups of siblings.

Step 11. Completed draft.

Step 12. Proceed with your lettering.

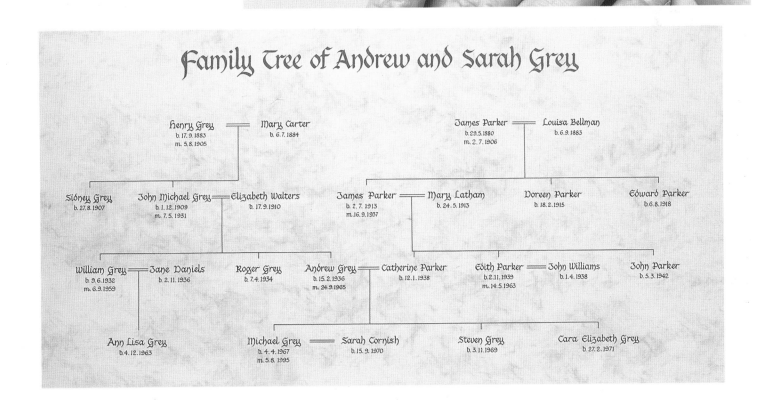

Large Family Trees

A larger, illustrated, genealogical chart is shown in Fig. 8. Although the steps used to build up the chart were exactly the same as those given above, remember that some very wide generations may be inherent in larger charts and that these will need to be compressed as much as possible in order to keep the whole piece within reasonable proportions. To assist the compression process, the names of couples can be arranged in a vertical block, with the line leading downward to the next generation being drawn directly below both partners' names (Fig. 9).

Try to keep each generation on a separate line, which will make the chart much easier to read. It may occasionally make better sense to fit a small family group between generations in order to simplify the layout, but if you do this too often you will lose the clear flow of generation following generation. If you need to make connecting lines cross over each other, use a small bridge (Fig. 10) so that it is obvious which line is going where.

Fig. 8. A large illustrated genealogy.

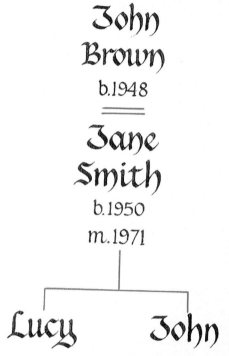

Fig. 9. Detail of vertical block of text.

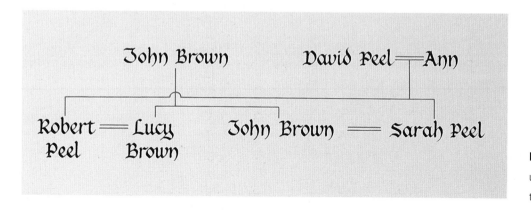

Fig. 10. Bridges can be used where lines cross to avoid confusion.

Rock Buns

4. Cream
ft. Add
ntil light
lour in very
ss mixture
- 20 minutes.
r sugar

403 self-raising flour
203 butter
203 sugar
1 egg
203 dried fruit

Rub fat into flour then
add sugar and half of
the egg then the dried
fruit. Mix all together
and place in spoonfuls
on a greased baking
tray. Cook for 15 minute
in oven at Reg. 4.

Blackletter 8

Blackletter

Blackletter—another Gothic lettering style dating from the Middle Ages—derives its name from the density of its upright strokes, the closer spacing of its letters, and the closer placing of its writing lines, all of which give it a much blacker appearance on the page than the more open styles that preceded it. This type of lettering accompanied many of the beautifully decorated and illuminated books of the medieval period. Although it was also used in some of the earliest printed books, it quickly lost ground to styles that were both easier to read and more practical for the printer to use.

Fig. 1. Blackletter practice strokes.

Begin learning this lettering style by practicing the strokes shown in Fig. 1. Because there are not many curved strokes in the blackletter hand, it suits calligraphers who have difficulty making uniformly rounded strokes, although care must be taken to get the spacing right so that the lettering does not look ugly.

The minuscule letters are illustrated in Fig. 2. Closely examine the construction of these letters and note that there are several terminations to the upright strokes and that each has a diagonal stroke attached to the beginning and end that is one of three different lengths (Fig. 3). As with the other alphabets, the "m" (Fig. 4) is a good example because it uses all three of these strokes in one letter. The first and last strokes are the short diagonal running straight into, or out of, the upright (Fig. 3). The bottom stroke of each of the first two uprights must be the small, centrally placed stroke illustrated in Fig. 3b; if you do not use this stroke you will close up the gaps between the uprights and make the letter difficult to read. The top two strokes connecting the three uprights are the slightly longer diagonal line that flows out of, or into, the upright (Fig. 3c). If you take care when forming these connecting strokes, the style will look even and well balanced.

The letter "a" starts with a long cross-stroke at a slight angle at the top, which leads into the downstroke and the final serif at the bottom. A thin, diagonal stroke is needed for the middle part of the letter to follow into the downstroke and the bottom stroke that connects with the bottom serif. To finish the letter, make a hairline connection between the top and the center of the letter, as illustrated in Fig. 5. Use the corner of the pen to make this stroke, which should be a natural curve leading round from one part of the letter to the other.

The top of the "d" should be carefully judged so that it finishes in the correct place to allow the second downward stroke to be the right distance from the first. The "e" is another letter that includes a thin, diagonal, connecting line, this time between the top stroke and the first upright stroke. A short, horizontal line can sometimes be taken from this stroke to the right, as is shown in Fig. 6, or else the stroke can be a diagonal line following the direction of the top stroke.

The "g," "j," and "y" are all similarly formed letters, whose tails are connected to the rest of the letter by means of a thin stroke. The stroke leading from the downstroke of the "j" begins where the vertical starts to bend to the right on a level with the bottom writing line.

abcdefghij

klmnopqr

stuvwxyz

Fig. 2. Blackletter minuscule alphabet.

Fig. 3. Terminations to upright strokes.

Fig. 4. The blackletter "m" contains the three different terminations to the upright strokes.

Fig. 5. Formation of letter "a."

Fig. 6. The letter "e."

The "s" is quite a difficult letter to write because it is formed by changing the pen direction many times (Fig. 7). The main strokes are then bisected by a thin, diagonal line running through the center, which should leave two tiny gaps on either side of the two middle strokes. You will have to adjust your pen very slightly when filling these. The "x," which is formed as shown in Fig. 8, has two central strokes that overlap each other.

Because the letters are written quite close together, and because so many of the strokes are the same, this style can be quite difficult to read. Some of the letters have variants (a few are shown in Fig. 9), however, whose use can make the hand both easier to read and more decorative. The final strokes of such letters as "h," "n," and "m" can be given an elongated, curving finish, for example, which breaks up a long row of uprights very well (Fig. 10). Similar curves, albeit at the top of the letters, can be added to the "v" and "w." You can find examples of all of these strokes in medieval manuscripts. A crosspiece can also be given to the central strokes of the "w" and "m" to make the letters a little clearer.

The capital letters of the blackletter alphabet are among the most decorative of any calligraphic hand (Fig. 11). As well as being quite complex, there are several versions of some letters —indeed, you can even embellish them further with extra strokes to suit your purposes. Nearly all of them have a thin, vertical stroke placed alongside an upright, and in order to make the thinnest possible stroke you will have to turn your pen completely sideways (Fig. 12). A small, extra stroke is often placed within the more open letters (Fig. 13). Because these letters are so decorative, however, words that consist solely of capitals are very difficult to read and tend to look fussy. If you are using the blackletter hand for titles, it is much better to combine the upper and lower cases instead, and to make the letters' increased size the dominant feature (Fig. 14).

The ascenders and descenders of the blackletter style can be given a very attractive finish by means of the fishtail, or Fraktur, serif shown in Fig. 15. The serif requires the same sort of hairline stroke that was used in the formation of cursive italic letters, which is made by using the corner of the pen to flick out the extra stroke (Fig. 16).

Fig. 7. The letter "s."

Fig. 8. The letter "x."

Fig. 9. Alternative letters.

Fig. 10. Using the more embellished letters to improve the legibility of a long row of vertical strokes.

Fig. 11. Blackletter capitals.

Fig. 12. The pen is held vertically for the thin strokes of the capital letters.

Fig. 13. A small additional stroke is often placed within the curved area for decoration.

Fig. 15. Fraktur serifs.

Fig. 16. The serif needs a deft manipulation of the corner of the nib.

Ye Olde Tea Shoppe

YE OLDE TEA SHOPPE

Fig. 14. A title in a mixture of blackletter minuscules and capitals is much easier to read than one composed of capitals only.

Making a Calendar

Numbers can be written to match the straight-sided, blackletter style, and these are shown in Step 1. Because they are not very easy to read, however, it is generally better to accompany most lettering styles with the simpler numerals of one of the plainer styles, for example, when you are writing an address, for which legibility is very important.

A simple, calligraphic calendar can be made using a heavy weight of paper or thin card. Write out the names of the seven days of the week in fairly large lettering (the examples shown in Step 2 were written with a nib size of 1). Write the months of the year in the same size, too, but in a different color. Leave plenty of space between each word because the cards will all be cut to the same size. Cut the cards so that each word is central (Step 3).

Write the numbers 1 to 31 with a larger nib (for the numbers illustrated in Step 4, a size 3 automatic pen was used, making figures about 1" (30mm) high).

Cut out all of the pieces of card to a height of 2 6/16" (60mm). The cards containing the weekday and month names should be cut to a width of 4 3/4" (120mm), and the numeral cards to a width of 2 6/16" (60mm).

You can display the day's date in various ways. Firstly, you could make a central hole at the top of each card and then hang the cards on a row of hooks fixed to a small board. You can buy suitable hooks from a hardware store. Secondly, you could make a simple stand out of thick, folded card, fashioning a lip at the bottom to hold the cards (Step 5).

A third alternative is to fix the cards into place on a board with strips of Velcro. Velcro (usually black or white), which is available from haberdashery stores, is composed of two strips of fabric that adhere to each other, but that can be pulled apart time and time again. Buy the "stick-and-stick" version, which is adhesive on the back of both strips, so that one piece can be applied to the back of a card and the other to the board (Step 6). If you look at the Velcro closely, you will see that one side is composed of tiny hooks and the other of a mesh of loops, to which the hooks catch. Use pieces of the hooked side of the strip for the cards and of the looped side for the display board. The board can then be hung up (Step 7).

Manufacturers of commercial display boards often cover them with a fabric that is designed for Velcro attachments, and you may be able to find such display boards and boxes of small, circular, Velcro fasteners in office-supply stores.

Step 1. Blackletter numbers.

Step 2. Write the weekdays and months in a large lettering size.

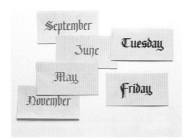

Step 3. The weekdays and months are centralized on the cut cards.

Step 4. The numbers 1 to 31 are written in foundation hand for clarity.

Step 5. A simple stand for the calendar cards is made from thick folded card.

Step 6. "Stick and stick" Velcro.

Step 7. A cord can be attached to the board for hanging.

Project
A Shakespeare Sonnet

Because the blackletter hand is very dense, a piece of text written in a block in this style looks very effective. The Shakespeare sonnet shown in Step 1 consists of lines of roughly the same length and therefore lends itself to this treatment.

Cutting and pasting text can be avoided with a layout like this because the lines are so similar in length that writing them out, line after line, as a straightforward practice piece will provide you with enough guidance for the final work and will also give you a good impression of how the finished piece will look in terms of its density of text, line spacing, and so on.

When you have written the draft text, measure the length of the lines (Step 2) to help you to make small adjustments to the starting point of each line to ensure that all of the lines are centered when you are writing the final piece. Any lines of text that are a little shorter than the majority can be indented slightly, making the difference in length less noticeable, while those that are slightly longer can be started slightly farther forward to give a square block of text. Now write out the text (Step 3). Because blackletter is written with only one letter height between each line of text, take care that you do not make the ascenders and descenders too long (Step 4).

The final piece was written on pale-blue Parchmarque paper in pairs of lines that were colored terre verte (a sage-green color), yellow ocher, and deep red. A size 3 Mitchell nib was used, and the writing lines, as well as the spacing between the lines, measured 1/4" (6mm). A dense piece of work like this needs a wide border, so allow for large margins around the text when you trim the paper to size.

Step 1. The text is written in draft and colored pencils indicate the chosen color scheme.

Step 2. Rule up the writing lines, then, using a central vertical line for measuring, mark the start and finish points of each line of text.

Step 3. Proceed with the lettering.

Step 4. Blackletter needs only one letter height between each pair of writing lines.

Making Borders

It is important to give some thought to the borders that will surround your work. Some examples are shown in Fig. 17. If you leave too little space for a border, the text will look as though it has been crammed on to the page. By contrast, if the borders are too large, the text may look a little lost. Good border proportions are usually achieved by allowing about a quarter of the width of the block of text for the side and top borders. The bottom border is generally made a little wider to give a balanced appearance.

Another Shakespeare sonnet is illustrated in Fig. 18. The initial letter has been enlarged for decorative purposes. If you allow a large initial letter to extend beyond the rest of the block of text, you could add a simple, colored, floral-patterned border down the left-hand edge (Fig. 19). By allowing the initial letter to protrude beyond the top line of the text you also can work the border along the top edge of the design, as well as down the left-hand side. By slightly shifting the block of text in relation to the page, you can furthermore either extend the border around three sides or make it completely surround the text.

You can also introduce small motifs and decorations to pieces that consist of several verses by placing these between the verses (Fig. 20 and Fig. 21). Alternatively, you could write the text within any suitable shape (Fig. 22). A framed piece is illustrated in Fig. 23.

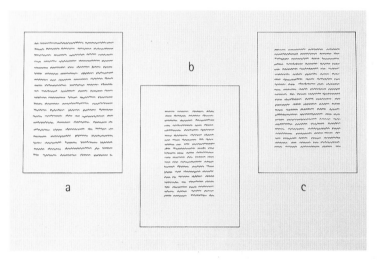

Fig. 17. Different border widths: a) too narrow, b) too wide, c) correct.

Fig. 18. A sonnet.

Fig. 19. Border construction.

Desiderium

My spirit longeth for Thee,
　　Within my troubled breast;
Although I be unworthy
　　Of so divine a Guest.

· · · ❧❧❧ · · ·

Of so divine a Guest,
　　Unworthy though I be;
Yet has my heart no rest,
　　Unless it come from Thee.

· · · ❧❧❧ · · ·

Unless it come from Thee,
　　In vain I look around;
In all that I can see,
　　No rest is to be found.

· · · ❧❧❧ · · ·

No rest is to be found,
　　But in Thy blessed love;
O! let my wish be crowned,
　　And send it from above!

John Byrom

Against Idleness and Mischief

How doth the little busy Bee　　　　How skilfully she builds her Cell!
Improve each shining Hour,　　　　How neat she spreads the Wax!
And gather Honey all the Day　　　　And labours hard to store it well
From ev'ry op'ning Flow'r!　　　　With the sweet Food she makes.

In Works of Labour or of Skill　　　　In Books, or Work, or healthful Play,
I would be busy too:　　　　Let my first Years be past,
For Satan finds some Mischief still　　　　That I may give for every Day
For idle Hands to do.　　　　Some good Account at last.

Isaac Watts

Fig. 20. Decoration between each verse embellishes this text.

Fig. 21. The verses can be arranged around a central decoration.

SOUND,
sound the clarion,
fill the fife! To all the
sensual world proclaim,
One crowded hour of
glorious life Is worth
an age without
a name.

Fig. 22. The text of this piece has been fitted into a circle.

Fig. 23. Two columns of text are separated by a central illustration.

Constructing a Recipe Book

The final project in this chapter is a recipe book, some of whose recipes have been written in draft. The title and list of ingredients for each recipe have been written in blackletter, while the cooking method is in italic.

If you want to create greater visual interest by varying the layout of the recipes from page to page, you could position blocks of text in ways that suit the quantity of text contained in each recipe. Step 1, for example, starts with a straightforward, centered title and then lists the ingredients in a block to the left, with the method being written on the right.

In Step 2, the ingredients have been split into two columns below the centered title, with the method occupying the entire width of both columns beneath them.

Because the list of ingredients illustrated in Step 3 is short, it has been placed under the title on the left-hand side of the page, with the method written in a block on the right to balance it.

Rock Buns

4 oz self-raising flour
2 oz butter
2 oz sugar
1 egg
2 oz dried fruit

Rub fat into flour then add sugar and half of the egg then the dried fruit. Mix all together and place in spoonfuls on a greased baking tray. Cook for 15 minutes in oven Reg. 4

Step 1. Here the title is centered, with ingredients to the left and method to the right.

Macaroons

2 egg whites   few drops almond essence
5 oz castor sugar   almonds or cherries
5 oz ground almonds   rice paper

Whisk egg white until very stiff. Add almond essence, then sugar and ground almonds. Roll the mixture into rounds and place - well spaced out - on rice paper. Put a cherry or almond on top of each biscuit Bake for 20 minutes at Reg.4 When nearly cold, remove from tin and tear around the rice paper.

Step 2. Here the ingredients are split into two columns, with a centered title and the method the width of both columns.

Shortbread

1 oz castor sugar
2 oz butter
3 oz plain flour

Preheat oven to Reg.4. Cream butter until very soft. Add sugar and cream until light and fluffy. Stir in flour in very small amounts. Press mixture into a tin. Cook for 20 minutes. Dredge with castor sugar while still hot.

Step 3. The title and ingredients are on the left, with the method on the right.

Step 4 shows a long list of ingredients centered down the page, with the method split into two columns to the left and right of them. The book can contain even more variants--to arrive at a good layout, regard the lettering as blocks of text that can be moved about the page and split into further blocks if necessary. This method of designing a page of text is useful for many types of work.

When you have decided on your layout, measure and rule the guidelines and marking points on your paper, and proceed with the lettering (Step 5).

The recipe book itself could either be a prebound book containing good-quality paper, or you could instead make and bind a simple book yourself. If you are making your own recipe book, first cut sheets of paper to form double-page spreads, allowing generous margins so that you can accommodate larger areas of text if necessary.

When you have a large enough collection of recipes (for example, six double-page spreads) to make a volume, bind them together with a title page and cover. You will need a thick, decorative paper for the cover. Alternatively, you could buy some purpose-made binding paper that has been strengthened with a mesh of fabric.

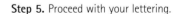

Florentines

Melt sugar and butter in pan. Add fruit, nuts and beaten egg, mix well. Grease baking trays and place tea-spoonfuls of mixture, well apart, on these. Cook for 10-15 mins. at top of oven, Reg. 3

4 oz castor sugar
4 oz butter
1 egg
3 oz chopped glacé cherries
3 oz raisins
2 oz chopped walnuts
4 oz plain chocolate

until golden brown. Remove from tray, with a palette knife, when nearly cold. Cool on wire trays. Melt chocolate and spread over one side of each biscuit.
Makes 25-30.

Step 4. The ingredients are centered down the page, with the method split into two columns.

4 oz self-raising flour
2 oz butter
2 oz sugar
1 egg
2 oz dried fruit

Step 5. Proceed with your lettering.

Step 6. A large needle and thick binding thread are needed.

Constructing a Recipe Book (Continued)

The pages are sewn together using binding thread and a large binding needle (Step 6). Sew them along the central crease through five evenly spaced marks as shown in Step 7. Push the needle through all of the sheets each time (Step 8). Bring the ends of the thread to the center of the pages and knot them together around the central thread (Step 9).

Step 7. This diagram indicates the direction the sewing thread should take.

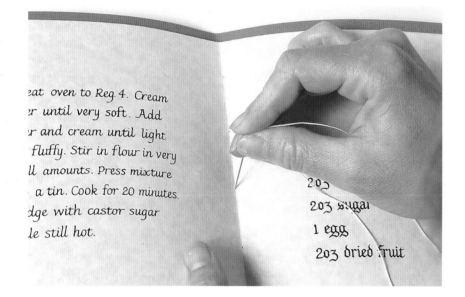

Step 8. Carefully sew the pages together.

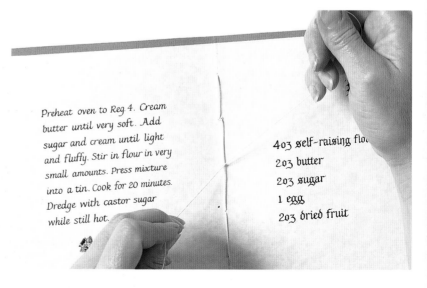

Step 9. Knot the ends around the central thread, then cut them off, leaving about an inch.

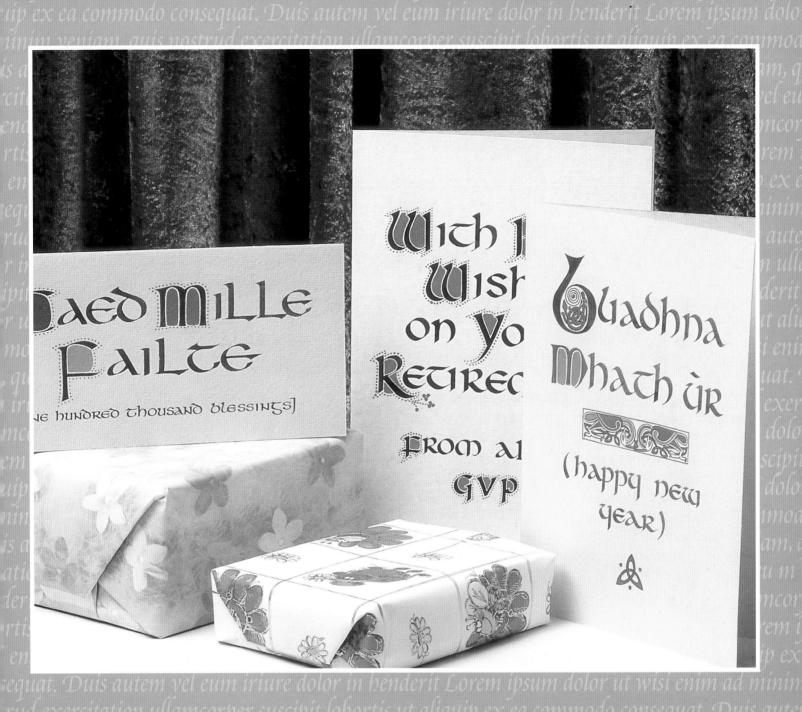

The Uncial Hand

The Uncial Hand

The uncial letters that can be seen in eighth- to tenth-century Celtic manuscripts have a squat, rounded appearance that can be useful for many types of decorative work. The letters are widely spaced, being closer to the round, or foundation, hand that we learned first than to the compressed styles that we subsequently moved on to.

Fig. 1. Modern uncial alphabet.

The letters shown in Fig. 1 are a simplified and modern form of the original uncial hands that were used during the Dark Ages. Because the letter height is slightly shallower than in most other styles, a height of four-and-a-half times the width of the nib will give a better effect than the normal five (Fig. 2). A slightly shallower pen angle is also required (Fig. 3).

The ascenders and descenders should be kept very short. In addition, as in the blackletter style, the height between the writing lines should be the height of one letter only (Fig. 4). In conjunction with the greater width of the letters, this will result in lettering that takes up a lot of space horizontally, but not vertically, so if you are writing a piece of text that contains a large number of short lines, this style will give the piece greater width.

The small, wedge-shaped serif of this hand is very easy to construct. The point that is given to the ascending strokes (Fig. 5) is simply a short, diagonal stroke taken to the left, and then to the right, before the downward stroke is begun. At the end of the horizontal stroke, the thickened, terminating stroke to such letters as "e," "f," and "l" is formed in a similar way, that is, by making another short stroke diagonally downward near to the end and then drawing the nib back up to the end of the horizontal to join the two strokes (Fig. 6).

The letter "a" begins with a diagonal stroke that is curved at each end to follow the natural direction of the pen. The narrow, loop shape that forms the rest of the letter is one continuous stroke that balances the diagonal. The "b," "c," "d," and "e" are all well-rounded letters. Remember, however, that when you are forming the top stroke of the "d" you should take care to bring it round to the correct position so that it completes the circle that was begun by its first stroke.

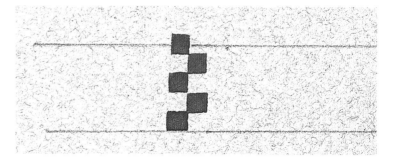

Fig. 2. The writing line height for uncials is 4.5 times the width of the nib.

Fig. 3. The pen is held at an angle of 20°.

The horizontal bar of the "f" extends slightly beyond the end of the top stroke, while the descending stroke finishes just below the bottom writing line. The "g" differs from the "c" only in having a slight tail at the bottom, which can be made without lifting the pen from the page after making the second rounded stroke. The "h" is usually given the rounded second stroke that is shown here, and care must be taken not to bring the final, trailing stroke too close to the first upright stroke, otherwise the letter will look like a "b."

Although the "i" and the "j" were not originally dotted, in order to make the lettering easier to read they can be given a thin, sideways stroke to form a "dot." The bottom of each of the aforementioned letters, as well as several others, is given a small serif in the form of another thin, sideways stroke, but in this case it should be less pronounced than that used for the "dot"—make it with little more than a diminishing flick of the pen. The "k" and the "r" are the same, apart from the lengthened first stroke of the "k." Because the squatness of these two letters can make them look quite cramped, and the looping second stroke and final diagonal are compressed into a small area, make sure that you write them as clearly as possible. The "l" has a bottom stroke that is the same length as the horizontal stroke of the "f."

An "m" formed with rounded outer strokes and an "n" with a rounded second stroke have been illustrated here, but remember that there are various alternatives to these two letters (some of which are shown below), any of which may be used in combination in a piece of lettering. When you are writing the rounded "n," do not take the end of the curved stroke too close to the vertical. A completely circular "o" is used, while the "p" is composed of only two strokes, with no extra small stroke joining the vertical to the rounded stroke. The end of the rounded stroke is carried around to meet the vertical, with the corner of the pen finishing the stroke. Although the rounded shape of the "v" is almost circular, the curve of the second stroke has been modified slightly, so that although there is a gap at the top, the second stroke still meets the first at the bottom in a matching curve that makes the letter look as though it were round.

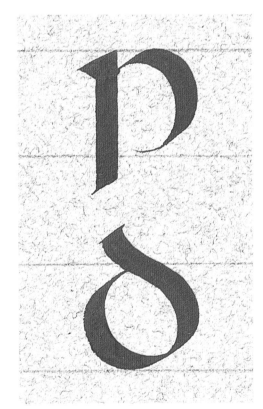

Fig. 4. Keep the ascenders and descenders short and allow one letter height between the writing lines.

Fig. 5. The small, wedge-shaped serif given to vertical strokes.

Fig. 6. The thick, terminating serif to horizontal strokes on the "e," "f," and "l."

Alternative Uncial Letters

Fig. 7 shows some of the alternative uncial letters that can be used in place of those given above. The unusually shaped "g" is more likely to be encountered in an original uncial alphabet, but because it is not very recognizable in a page of text, you will need to decide whether clarity or authenticity is more important to the particular piece of lettering that you are working on. Note that the "l" illustrated here has the same curve as that used for first stroke of the "b" in the letters shown here.

The alternative "y" is not found in Celtic manuscripts, but is shown here because it can be helpful when you want the text to be very legible (the version given above can closely resemble a "u" at first glance).

Fig. 7. Some alternative uncial letters.

Fig. 8. Angular capital letters often found accompanying uncials.

Enlarged Minuscules

Uncial text did not contain capital letters at the beginning of sentences. Where it was necessary to place emphasis on particular letters, an enlarged version of the minuscule was used instead, often with a little extra embellishment of color and decoration. Large, very angular letters can be found in groups in some Celtic manuscripts, and these can be used as capital letters. Because they were usually drawn and painted rather than being written with a pen, however, their shapes do not lend themselves to being written as part of an ordinary block of text (Fig. 8).

The enlarged versions of the minuscule letters are made with a nib of the same size as that used for the rest of the text, but are built up with several stokes of the pen to create the extra weight needed for their increased height. If you have trouble with these large-sized letters, work on them on layout paper until you have formed a pleasingly shaped letter. You can then trace the outline of this letter and use the tracing as a guide, either for subsequent letters or for your final pieces, until you have become proficient enough to write them freehand. Fig. 9 shows an alphabet of letters based on Celtic-manuscript uncials that can be used as capitals.

The Irish saying (with its translation) shown in Fig. 10 is a typical uncial text, with larger, lightly illuminated letters scattered over the page. The centers of the large letters, as well as the spaces around them, were filled with another color and then surrounded by red dots (Fig. 11). Fig. 12 shows another example of uncial lettering that was used to make a retirement card.

The original uncial letters were written with the pen held at very flat angle (fig.13). If you look at old manuscripts, however, you will see that it would not have been possible for the scribe strictly to adhere to a constant pen angle when producing some of the strokes, so you can use a little latitude when writing this alphabet. Indeed, there are many variants to some of the letters, which nevertheless retain a Celtic feeling.

ABCDE
FGhIJK
LMNOP
QRSTU
VWXYZ

Fig. 9. Large uncials used as capitals.

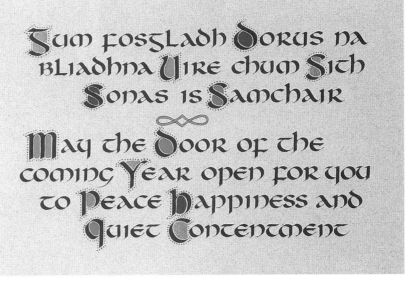

Fig. 10. An Irish text scattered with lightly illuminated letters.

Fig. 11. The letter is filled with a color and surrounded with red dots.

With Best
Wishes
on Your
Retirement

From all at

GVP

Fig. 12. A retirement card.

Fig. 13. An eighth-century uncial alphabet.

Project

Designing a Celtic Greeting Card

We will now make a greeting card that features the well-known Irish saying *Caed Mille Failte* ("One-hundred-thousand blessings"). You will need a fairly stiff card of at least 150gsm (grams per square meter) for this project.

Because you will probably want it to fit into an envelope, the card has been designed with dimensions of around 9 x 4" (210 x 105mm). Not only are there plenty of envelopes available in this size, but it will also suit the wording very well.

Because the design includes few words, you will need a large-sized nib. Experiment a little until you have found the best size (Step 1). Here, a size 1 1/2 nib was first used, which worked quite well. Since there was still plenty of unfilled space on the card,

however, the lettering was then written with a size 1 nib. Not only did the lettering produced also fit within the required space, but it also had a bolder, more striking appearance. The size 1 nib was therefore chosen over the size 1 1/2 (Step 2).

Write out and center the smaller lettering of the translation (Step 3). A size 4 nib was used here, with the writing lines about 3/16" (4mm) apart. This size seemed ideal, so no further experimentation was needed.

Now decide on the decoration. In this example, the three initials will be given the simple, filled center and surround of dots that was mentioned above (Step 4).

Cut the card to size--about 9 x 9" (210 x 210mm)--and leave it unfolded while you are working on the lettering (it is easier to

measure the writing lines accurately from a straight, cut, top edge rather than from a slightly uneven, doubled-over edge).

Work out the position that the text will occupy on the bottom portion of the unfolded card and rule in the writing lines (Step 5).

Step 6: write the text and then decorate it. (Always leave the decoration until the text has been written in case you make an error that may necessitate you having to start again.)

Fold the card, matching up the corners carefully, and crease it slightly. Use a bone folder to finish the crease, which will give you a crisp, sharp fold. The finished card is shown in Step 7.

Step 1. Choosing the best nib size.

Step 2. Experimenting with an alternative nib.

Step 3. Add the small lettering.

Step 4. Add the decoration.

Step 5. Measure and rule the writing lines on the unfolded card.

Step 6. Use a bone folder to give a crisp fold to the card.

Step 7. The finished card.

Celtic Decorative Motifs

A Celtic new-year greetings-card design is illustrated in Fig. 14. (*Bliadhna Mhath-ur* means "Happy New Year.")

Celtic manuscripts abound in wonderful motifs with which to decorate texts: knotwork patterns interwoven with animals and birds can be used to enliven any piece of lettering, for example, and many good sourcebooks feature illustrations from such great Celtic manuscripts as the Book of Kells and the Lindisfarne Gospels.

Fig. 14. A new year greetings card.

Project

Celtic Birthday Card

The design for the birthday card pictured in Step 1 was arrived at by first writing the lettering in uncials, using large initial letters for each word. When centered beneath one another on the draft (Step 2), the three words suggested a square, rather than a rectangular, shape for the card, and because the corners were obvious areas to decorate, an outer pattern of Celtic knotwork that concentrated on these areas was decided upon. One corner was first designed using a linear pattern (Step 3), which was repeated in each corner (Step 4), the corners then being joined with twisting bands to form a complete border. The card used was Marlmarque.

Step 1. A Celtic knotwork card.

Step 2. The centered words suggest the overall proportions of the card.

Step 3. Beginning of the linear pattern.

Step 4. The border is a repeat pattern of each corner.

Paper and Card for Calligraphy

Paper and card for calligraphy need to have various suitable characteristics, the most important being surface texture. Paper that is not porous enough will result in the ink sitting on the surface and not penetrating the fibers properly. Although the ink will dry after some time, the letters are unlikely to be sharp and clear. By contrast, paper that is too porous will cause the ink to spread among the fibers like blotting paper, and crisp, sharp-edged letters will again not be produced. Two very good papers that have just the right degree of absorbency are the Fabriano Ingres and Arches papers (Fig. 15). Others that you may be able to find locally are T.H. Saunders, Waterford, and Canson papers. Such papers are usually sold in large sheets, and the Fabriano Ingres and Canson papers come in a wide range of colors (Fig. 16), as well as a choice of thicknesses.

Apart from its absorbency, the correct surface texture is also important because some papers can be quite rough, in which case the nib may catch on any loose fibers, resulting in either a spatter of ink across the page or badly formed letters. This is less of a problem when you are using larger nib sizes than those numbering from 3 to 6. Although you can sometimes use a rough texture to your advantage, in that you can produce an interesting effect, a fairly smooth surface is generally preferable.

When you are buying handmade papers, you will find that they are described according to their surface texture. "Rough" papers have been pressed between sheets of felt before being dried, with the result that the texture of the felt is impressed onto the paper. "Not" papers are smoother, because the sheets are pressed together several times, while "hot-pressed" (H.P.) papers are given a much smoother surface by being pressed between hot metal plates.

When paper is made, a pulp consisting of its fibers is shaken in a large tray until the pulp is evenly spread over the whole surface of the tray. In the case of handmade paper, the fibers end up lying in a more random manner, which gives a less pronounced general direction to the fibers than when they are shaken by machine, which produces less variation in movement. The dominant direction of the fibers will give the paper a more pronounced grain direction when it has dried. This can be seen when a sheet of paper is torn: the tear produced across the grain is far more jagged than a tear made along the grain, that is, in the same direction as the fibers. Remember this when you are cutting paper and card—perhaps for greeting cards—as not only is it easier to fold, but you will also achieve a neater, sharper crease when folding along the grain rather than against it.

A laid surface can be given to the paper by making it in trays whose wire mesh has a more pronounced pattern. Watermarks are similarly produced, in that the wires are

Fig. 15. Some good papers for calligraphy: Arches Aquarelle, Canson Mi-Teintes, Fabriano Ingres, Fabriano 5, and Waterford.

Fig. 16. A selection of the Canson and Ingres paper colors.

Fig. 17. Vellum-effect papers: real vellum, Parchmarque, Pergamenata (vegetable parchment), and Elephanthide.

Fig. 18. Textured and patterned papers: Ingres pastel paper, mottled green; Canson Mi-teintes, mottled dark gray and light gray; Countryside; Kashmir; Marlmarque in a range of colors; Cloud Nine paper in six colors; hammer embossed; linen embossed.

Fig. 19. A selection of Japanese papers.

formed into a specific shape. Because fewer fibers lie on the raised parts of the wire's design, a variation in surface texture that corresponds to the shape of the wires is produced when the paper is turned out of the tray.

Paper thickness is measured in grams per square meter (gsm). The average writing or office-stationery paper weighs between 90 and 110gsm, which is rather thin for calligraphy because it is likely to crinkle when it is dampened by ink and paint. A good weight for most calligraphic lettering is 150gsm. If you require card, you will find that 300gsm is a fairly stiff weight that will stand up on its own.

The durability of the paper could be an important factor when you are planning a piece of lettering. If you want to ensure that your paper will not deteriorate too quickly, look for an acid-free, conservation-grade paper. Most good paper stores will be able to tell you the acid content of their papers and advise you on which to choose.

Paper manufacturers have long been trying to produce acceptable substitutes for vellum and parchment, writing surfaces that are very good for lettering. Not only can mistakes be fairly easily removed from these animal skins, but their veining can look very attractive, too. Some of the papers that have been made in an effort to reproduce some, or all, of these qualities are shown in Fig. 17. All are very good-quality papers, with different characteristics.

A selection of colored papers that have different textures and patterns, such as a mottled or marbled effect, are pictured in Fig. 18. Japanese paper manufacturers produce some very attractive, decorative papers, some of which are shown in Fig. 19. Many are suitable for lettering and can add a lot to your designs. Woodgrain paper, which is available in a large range of colors, has a surface that is perfect for lettering. And although some of the lace- or string-effect papers can be more challenging, they can also be written upon successfully.

Seating Plan

Top Table
Mr. Timothy Dodds
Mrs. Patricia Edwards
Mr. James Collinson
Mrs. Georgina Edwards
Mr. Simon Edwards
Mrs. Anthea Collinson
Mr. Anthony Edwards
Miss Chloe Webb

Table 2
Miss Connie Partridge
Mr. Andrew Good
Mrs. Pauline Collinson
Mr. Reg Collinson
Mrs. Sandra Gains
Mr. Peter Gains
Miss Helen Gains
Mr. Alan Westbrook

Table 3
Miss Sylvia Porritt
Mr. Jason Stock
Mrs. Lynne Edwards
Mr. Norman Edwards
Miss Janine Edwards
Master Ryan Edwards
Master Daniel Edwards
Mrs. Edith Edwards

Table 4
Mr. David Collinson
Mrs. Linda Collinson
Mr. Kevin Collinson
Miss Susie Galloway
Mr. James Jell
Mrs. Lorna Jell
Mr. William Collinson
Miss Carla Stenning

Table 5
Mr. Gary Markham
Mrs. Angela Markham
Mr. Jim Lowe
Mrs. Tanya Lowe
Miss Dana Lowe
Master Peter Lowe
Mrs. June Rawlings
Mr. Thomas Gardener

Table 6
Mr. George Edwards
Mrs. Katherine Trabbett
Mr. Brian Wilson
Mrs. Gina Wilson
Mr. Roger Edwards
Mrs. Corinne Edwards
Mr. David Banks
Mrs. Linda Banks

Table 7
Mr. Thomas Collinson
Mrs. Wendy Collinson
Mr. Simon Collinson
Ms. Tina Denning
Mr. William Allott
Mrs. June Allott
Mr. James Allott
Miss Petra Trent

Table 9
Mr. Graham Pask
Miss Fiona
Mr.
Miss Lyn
Mr.

Mr & Mrs James Collinson
request the pleasure of the company of

Mr & Mrs G. Markham

at the marriage of their daughter

Georgina

to

Mr. Simon David Edwards

on Saturday 15th July 2000 at 2 pm
&
St Andrew's Church, Lamesley
and afterwards at the Welton Grange Hotel

R.S.V.P.

Copperplate Lettering

The final lettering style that we shall learn is copperplate, which printers usually call palace script, or just script. This is the style that is most commonly associated with invitations and wedding stationery, and is also useful for filling in the blank spaces of a form or certificate that has been printed in copperplate (Fig. 1). If you need to write on a preprinted card such as this, make sure that it will take the ink acceptably, as some printed cards can be quite shiny and unabsorbent. When removing any writing lines, be especially careful not to smudge the ink, which may have dried on the surface of the paper without penetrating the fibers sufficiently and could therefore be removed more easily than you expect.

Copperplate was also the hand that was used for writing official documents during the eighteenth, nineteenth, and early twentieth centuries, and many old vellum deeds can be seen that are inscribed in beautiful copperplate handwriting. Indeed, certain longstanding establishments still continue to write some of their prestigious documents in this way.

Copperplate Lettering

Of all of the lettering styles, copperplate is the least forgiving of error and needs a great deal of practice to master. The nib required to write this hand is different from the broad-edged nib that we have used for all of the other styles that we have learned, in that it has a thin point (Fig. 2). The William Mitchell copperplate nib also has an elbow bend to make it easier to use. No reservoir is required, as quite a few of the letters can be written each time that you dip the nib into the ink. Take care not to press down on the nib too heavily as you make your strokes, however, or else its fine points will splay apart and the ink will not flow from it properly.

There is no need for a range of nib sizes for copperplate lettering because the same nib makes all of the lettering sizes, as illustrated in Fig. 3. As you can see, in the case of the smaller lettering heights, a difference of half a millimeter in the width of the writing lines can make quite a difference to the lettering size. The angle of slope of the letters is about 45°, but you can vary the angle to suit your own preference to acertain extent,

Fig. 1. Copperplate lettering on a printed certificate.

the only requirement being that you keep whichever degree of slope you choose constant throughout the piece of lettering.

The basic copperplate alphabet is shown in Fig. 4. The main difficulty that this hand will give you is keeping the constant degree of slope to the words, and if this causes you real problems, use diagonal guidelines, as well as your normal writing lines, to ensure that you keep the angle constant (Fig. 5). The height between the writing lines should be at least two letter heights, and three or four letter heights can often look better because the ascending and descending strokes are long, elaborate flourishes (Fig. 6).

Fig. 2. The copperplate nib.

two millimetres
two and a half
three millimetres
three and a half
four millimetres
four and a half
five millimetres
six millimetres
seven millimetres
eight millimetres

Fig. 3. Different lettering sizes can be written with the same nib.

a b c d e f g

h i j k l m n

o p q r s t u v

w x y z

Fig. 4. Copperplate minuscules.

the flowers of

the

Fig. 5. Text with diagonal guidelines behind to help maintain a constant angle of slope to the letters.

the quick brown

fox jumps over

the lazy dog

Fig. 6. Lines of copperplate text with three times the writing-line height between each pair of lines.

The difference between this style and those that are written with a broad-edged pen is that you form the letters with fewer lifts of the pen from the paper. The nib can be moved backward where necessary, giving the style an attractive fluidity. Words are written in continuous streams, with only the occasional break being taken to cross or dot letters like "t" or "i." Because the nib point is so fine, you will need to write on a fairly smooth-surfaced paper, as one with too much texture will not enable the pen to glide freely over the surface and thus create the hand's long, smoothly flowing strokes.

In their simplest form, the ascending strokes are broad and blunt-ended. Letters never commence from the top of an ascending stroke; instead the pen is first taken upward in a sweeping stroke from the left, as if it were coming from another letter. Where the pen stops and then begins the downward stroke, a neat, squared end is made (Fig. 7). When you become more proficient in this style, you could try giving the uprights looped ascenders (Figs. 8 to 10). The larger your lettering, the easier it is to produce looped ascenders and descenders, and the more they complement the writing (see the (5/16"- (8mm-) high letters in Fig. 3 on page 117). When making the looped ascenders, the pen stroke from the left sweeps farther across before looping back to make the letter's downstroke.

The linking of copperplate letters is vital if the rhythm and flow of the words are to be maintained. Each letter is linked by a fine stroke leading from the bottom right of the previous letter to the top left of the new letter. Where there is no natural connecting stroke—as with such letters as "r" and "s," which finish with the pen in the wrong position to start the next letter—a break in the flow is necessitated, the next letter commencing with an initial sweeping stroke from the left (Fig. 11). Alternatively, versions of some of the letters (Fig. 12) can be formed to include a connecting stroke.

The letter "f" may cause you problems, as the central crossbar is often formed with a continuous linking stroke leading from the bottom loop to the crossbar (Fig. 13). The descender having been formed, the pen either sweeps backward to run up to the crossbar or forward to make the bottom loop, before crossing back over the descending stroke to form the crossbar. The "k" can be given either a looped or straight second stroke (Fig. 14). It is also possible to make rounded and curved versions of the "v" and "w," while the "z" has both a normal and a tailed version.

The capital letters for the copperplate hand are shown in Fig. 15. Some alternatives are shown in Fig. 16. These can be greatly embellished to make them attractive, illuminated letters with which to accompany texts (Fig. 17).

Fig. 7. Squared ends to the ascenders.

Fig. 8. Looped ends to the ascenders.

Fig. 9. Keep the height of the ascenders constant.

a b c d e f g h
i j k l m n o p
q r s t u r w x
y z

Fig. 10. The complete alphabet, with looped ascenders and descenders.

Fig. 11. Connecting strokes for difficult letters.

Fig. 12. Some letters can be formed differently to incorporate a connecting stroke.

Fig. 13. Two versions of the letter "f."

Fig. 14. A few other alternative letters.

Fig. 15. The capital letters.

Fig. 16. Alternative versions of some capitals.

Fig. 17. Embellished capitals.

Making a Wedding-invitation Card

When making a wedding-invitation card, first make a rough draft of the lettering to the size and shape required, emphasizing the most important lines of text: the names and places (Step 1).

Start by guessing the sizes of lettering that will look best, and then cut and paste the alternative versions until you have achieved the best combination (Step 2).

When you are happy with your draft, measure and rule the guidelines and marked points onto your chosen card and proceed with your lettering (Step 3).

Step 1. Wedding-invitation card draft.

Step 2. The cut-and-pasted draft.

Step 3. Proceed with the lettering.

Project
Addressing Envelopes

Before addressing envelopes, first make a template so that you won't have to rule a set of writing lines on each. Carefully measure and cut a piece of card to the size of the envelope so that the card fits quite snugly inside it (Step 1). This will prevent the card from shifting slightly and displacing the lines.

Lettering with a height of about ⅛" (3mm) is about the right size for most envelopes. Six sets of writing lines will

suffice for most addresses. Rule up your writing lines on the card, leaving about 5/16" (7mm) between each pair in the central portion of the envelope. Allow a reasonable margin at the top- and left-hand sides.

Step in each line by an equal amount. For smaller, squarer sizes of envelope (Step 2), step in each line by about about 3/16" (5mm). For a longer envelope (Step 3), step in the lines at about 7/16" (10mm) intervals to

make better use of the area available.

Rule in the guidelines, making them quite thick so that they will show through the envelope (Step 4).

If an address has only four lines of text, start writing it on the second pair of lines so that the lettering will be more centrally positioned on the envelope (Step 5).

Step 1. Make a template for addressing small envelopes.

Step 2. On a small envelope, each address line is stepped in by 3/16" (5mm).

Step 3. The address lines are stepped in 7/16" (10mm) on longer envelopes.

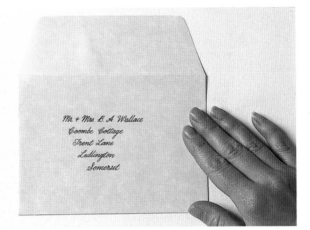

Step 4. The lines should be thick enough to be seen through the envelope.

Step 5. Short addresses should be started at the second pair of lines on the template.

Making a Seating Plan

Step 1. Calculate the text size needed for the size of mount board.

Step 2. Proceed with the lettering.

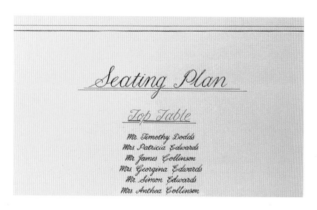

Step 3. A simple border can be added in matching colors.

Step 4. A ruling pen is used for the border.

Our next project is a seating plan, which has to be quite large so that several people can see it at once when it is on display. If it needs to be freestanding, write it on mount board, which has a good surface for calligraphy and is available from most art stores in a wide range of colors.

Arrange the tables of guests—11 in the example shown—on your draft in the same position in which they will be placed in the dining room.

Use a lettering size that will allow you to fit all of the text within the board that you are using. The mount board sold by art stores is usually about about 23¾" x 33⅝" (60 x 85cm) (Step 1), but you may be able to buy larger pieces from picture-framers.

Write the guests' names and the title (Step 2). Given the quantity of guests in this example, lettering about 1/8" (3mm) high was needed to fit in all of the names without making the text appear too cramped. The title was written with 7/16"- (10mm-) high lettering to balance the rest of the text.

Add a simple border (Step 3) to decorate the design. This is made with a ruling pen (Step 4).

Mounting, Framing, and Care

11

Mounting, Framing, and Care

As you progress to working on more complex pieces, and spend more time and trouble on them, you will probably reach the stage where you want to frame a piece. When you take your work to be framed, consider asking the picture-framer to mount it, which can greatly improve the appearance of many pieces (Fig. 1). Not only are picture-framers used to advising people, but they generally also know what will look right, so it is worth asking for their advice. The range of colored mount boards that picture-framers stock is usually very extensive, which means that you should be able to choose one that will either match or complement the colors in your work. The picture-framer will cut the mount with a beveled edge (Fig. 2), and can also rule in extra lines of color near the edge of the mount if you wish, which adds further to the overall effect (Fig. 3).

Fig. 1. A simple mount can improve a piece if it is to be framed.

Whether or not it will have a mount, always give your piece ample margins so that it does not look as though it has been squashed into its frame (Fig. 4). If you are planning a piece for a particular wall space in a house, you will need to take into account how much its overall size will be increased by its frame and mount.

For the frame, you will be offered a wide range of moldings, mainly gold colors or varnished, or polished, natural woods. In addition, an increasing number of frames with colored moldings, as well as stained and painted effects, are becoming available, so you will have many options to choose from. The sample frames take the form of corner sections, which you can hold against the work, along with a corner piece of mount board, to get good impression of the final effect (Fig. 5).

The picture-framer will probably offer you the choice of reflective or nonreflective glass (Fig. 6). Although nonreflective glass has a slight texture, which prevents the light from shining back at the viewer, a degree of clarity is lost because the glass slightly reduces the sharpness and overall brightness of the work. You will need to balance this disadvantage against the possibility that the work will be hung in a position where the light will be shining directly onto it, thereby making it difficult to view without looking at it from many different angles. Note that it is generally better to hang calligraphic works in positions that do not receive direct sunlight because this will age the surface and can also bleach many colors as time goes by.

As you will appreciate, you will have to make a lot of compromises when having your work framed, and it is therefore worth weighing up all of the options in advance to enable you to choose the best solution for your requirements.

Calligraphic Inspirations

In order to build upon some of the projects that you have learned in this book, you cannot do better than to examine historical examples of calligraphy. The British Library in London, England, displays many fine, medieval manuscripts in cabinets, including the Lindisfarne Gospels—one of the best-known examples of calligraphy. The Bedford Psalter is also worth looking at on account of its fine illumination. Arabic manuscripts usually contain some stunning color schemes accompanying their distinctive texts, and you can also draw on pieces from many other countries for inspiration. You can often buy postcards and books featuring such exhibits that you can study at home at your leisure.

Look out for exhibitions of the work of contemporary scribes, which may give you fresh ideas for calligraphic execution and presentation.

Fig. 2. Beveled edge to a mount.

Fig. 3. Colored border lines around the aperture.

Fig. 4. The first of these examples has margins that are too small, the second has correctly proportioned margins.

Fig. 5. Corner pieces of frame and mount are useful for deciding which combination to use.

Fig. 6. Reflective and nonreflective glass.

Index

Acknowledgments

The author and publisher would like to thank the following:

Mr Window

for permission to reproduce the large family tree on p.92

Mrs Angela Lynskey

for creating the flower display shown on p.115.